"Even the most intelligent people struggle with relationships. This groundbreaking book reveals that the way our brain is wired causes us to make many bad decisions in our relationships. All of us are susceptible to subtle decision-making errors called *cognitive biases*, which can devastate our social ties with our loved ones, our friends, our coworkers, our local community, and our society as a whole.

Gleb Tsipursky combines cutting-edge research and pragmatic case studies to show the kind of problems that result from falling into these mental blindspots. More importantly, *The Blindspots Between Us* offers science-based strategies that anyone can adopt immediately to address the problems caused by cognitive biases in their relationships, helping their relationships not only survive, but thrive."

—**Scott Barry Kaufman, PhD**, scientific director
of The Imagination Institute at the University of
Pennsylvania, author of *Ungifted*, coauthor of *Wired
to Create*, host of *The Psychology Podcast*, and writer for
the column "Beautiful Minds" for *Scientific American*

"Do not buy this book on impulse. Your gut cannot be trusted. But I hope you will trust *me* when I say, objectively, that you should buy this book. It has a high probability of improving your life—and your relationships—immensely. It will help you avoid cognitive biases. Whether you're a student or a CEO, it will aid you in making better decisions about dating, family, friends, money, work, dessert—you name it."

—**A. J. Jacobs**, author of four *New York Times*
bestsellers, including *The Know-It-All*;
and editor at *Esquire* magazine

"Our ability to enter into, nourish, and at times even end relationships in healthy ways is one of the keys to living a happy and fulfilling life. Yet most of us struggle with painful relational patterns that show up again and again, thwarting our ability to realize the higher potentials our relationships hold for well-being and mutual satisfaction. In this well-written, well-researched offering, Gleb Tsipursky provides clear and effective ways to relate to one another that promise to empower our relationships to be healthier and happier for many years to come. I strongly recommend it to those of us who are committed to learning how to grow our ability to love and be loved."

—**Katherine Woodward Thomas**, *New York Times* bestselling author of *Conscious Uncoupling* and *Calling in "The One"*; and licensed marriage and family therapist

"Let's face it—our brains are lazy. We're almost always looking for the easiest solution to a problem or the quickest answer to a question. Thinking carefully about anything is a lot of work. That's what makes Gleb Tsipursky's book so valuable. He clearly explains how our thinking shortcuts work, and when it's time to step back and give something a little more thought. Bad decisions can harm us at work and in our personal relationships, and Tsipursky's book is the only one I know of that addresses how cognitive biases affect our relationships—and believe me, I've read many books on cognitive biases. Tsipursky bases his work on the latest cognitive science research, and yet makes it very down-to-earth. A very enjoyable, revealing read."

—**Michael Britt, PhD**, host of *The Psych Files* podcast, professor emeritus at Marist College, and best-selling author of *Psych Experiments*

"Trusting my gut led to two less-than-ideal marriages, and even an affair. I convinced myself it was okay because my body was 'speaking' to me. In hindsight, this was not healthy behavior. Once logic took over, I could see my actions were damaging to me and the people around me. Gleb Tsipursky's book will keep you from making the same mistakes as me."

—**Gabe Howard**, best-selling author of *Mental Illness Is an Asshole*, and host of *The Psych Central Podcast*

"Maybe I'm biased, but this is a terrific book! Cognitive bias is a significant and ever-present challenge in all our lives. Our mental biases color our perceptions, blind us to opportunity, narrow our options, and even force us into mistaken courses of action. But it doesn't have to be that way. Gleb Tsipursky offers a deeply coherent system for understanding our biases and then debiasing them ourselves. The book manages to be both wide ranging in scope and strategic in presentation, as it builds from start to finish, and provides meaningful exercises along the way for integrating the lessons. Readers' lives will be dramatically improved, so I highly recommend reading it!"

—**Rick Kirschner, PhD**, best-selling coauthor of *Dealing with People You Can't Stand*, and author of *How to Click with People*

"A fascinating book! In today's complex world, we still base too many relationships and big decisions on our gut instincts—and then wonder what went wrong. Gleb Tsipursky has a road map (and the experience to go with it!) for 'debiasing' our thinking for much better results. I'm going to keep this book close by as a reference when I know I need to check myself."

—**Bill Eddy**, best-selling author of 5 *Types of People Who Can Ruin Your Life* and *Why We Elect Narcissists and Sociopaths—and How We Can Stop*

"We assumed this book would be useful, and it is. What we were surprised by is how intellectually engaging and entertaining it is; not only to read, but to discuss and apply with friends, colleagues, and family."

—**Sheila Heen and Douglas Stone**, coauthors of *Difficult Conversations* and *Thanks for the Feedback*

"Gleb Tsipursky's take on how cognitive blindspots damage relationships is fresh, creative, and backed by solid research. He offers entertaining examples of how friends and families fall out due to egocentricity, tribalism, superiority, and other biases. Then he offers ample exercises to help you identify and overcome your blindspots to achieve the empathy and close connection you crave with your loved ones. This book is a real gem."

—**Patrick Fanning**, best-selling author and coauthor of eight self-help books, including *Couple Skills* and *Mind and Emotions*

"The root causes of most relationship discord begin hundreds of thousands of years ago on the African savannah, where quick emotional reflexes were often lifesaving. Today, however, these same emotional reflexes tend to trap couples in endless, unproductive cycles of anger, fault-finding, and blame. Gleb Tsipursky masterfully applies the new brain science behind *Thinking, Fast and Slow* to show how slow, deliberate thinking can be the master key to avoiding the emotional traps that bedevil so many relationships. What's more, he's stocked this book with simple, actionable advice for turning resolutions into reality. Any intelligent modern couple, no matter how well-adjusted, will find much value in this book. As a therapist, I've always found it paradoxical that most of my interventions with clients involved helping them be less emotional with each other. After reading *The Blindspots Between Us*, now I know why."

—**Stephen Snyder, MD**, best-selling author of
Love Worth Making, host of *The Relationship Doctor*
podcast on Macmillan Publishers' QDT Network,
and associate clinical professor of psychiatry at the
Icahn School of Medicine at Mount Sinai

THE BLIND SPOTS BETWEEN US

How to Overcome Unconscious Cognitive Bias & Build Better Relationships

Gleb Tsipursky, PhD

New Harbinger Publications, Inc.

Publisher's Note

This publication is designed to provide accurate and authoritative information in regard to the subject matter covered. It is sold with the understanding that the publisher is not engaged in rendering psychological, financial, legal, or other professional services. If expert assistance or counseling is needed, the services of a competent professional should be sought.

In consideration of evolving American English usage standards, and reflecting a commitment to equity for all genders, "they/them" is used in this book to denote singular persons.

Distributed in Canada by Raincoast Books

Copyright © 2020 by Gleb Tsipursky
New Harbinger Publications, Inc.
5674 Shattuck Avenue
Oakland, CA 94609
www.newharbinger.com

Cover design by Sara Christian; Acquired by Elizabeth Hollis Hansen; Edited by Gretel Hakanson

Library of Congress Cataloging-in-Publication Data

Names: Tsipursky, Gleb, author.
Title: The blindspots between us : how to overcome unconscious cognitive bias and build better relationships / Gleb Tsipursky.
Description: Oakland, CA : New Harbinger Publications, [2020] | Includes bibliographical references.
Identifiers: LCCN 2019055194 (print) | LCCN 2019055195 (ebook) | ISBN 9781684035083 (paperback) | ISBN 9781684035090 (pdf) | ISBN 9781684035106 (epub)
Subjects: LCSH: Judgment--Psychological aspects. | Cognition. | Decision making. | Interpersonal relations.
Classification: LCC BF447 .T78 2020 (print) | LCC BF447 (ebook) | DDC 158.2--dc23
LC record available at https://lccn.loc.gov/2019055194
LC ebook record available at https://lccn.loc.gov/2019055195

Printed in the United States of America

22   21   20

10   9   8   7   6   5   4   3   2   1   First Printing

This book is dedicated to my wife, best friend, and life partner, Agnes, with whom I have the most important relationship in my life.

Contents

Foreword   vii

Introduction   1

1   Autopilot vs. Intentional   7

2   Our Attribution Errors   39

3   Are We Really Better?   59

4   The Danger of Tribalism   79

5   Feeling, Thinking, and Talking Past Each Other   95

6   The Importance of Caring   113

7   The Glass Is Half…   125

8   (Don't) Tell Me What to Do!   141

9   Communicating Rationally   155

Conclusion: Helping Others Spot Their Blindspots   169

Acknowledgments   173

Glossary   175

Endnotes   181

Foreword

You may have noticed that there's a panic in the air when it comes to writing about human psychology. There's a pessimism that has slipped into our hearts and our words. Among those who describe what is wrong with our thinking, there are too few experts prescribing what can be done about it. That's why this book is different. That's why this book is important.

Over the last decade or so, many books detailing our irrationality have made their way into bookstores and airports. They've been bestsellers. They've changed the way we think, feel, and talk about ourselves. We've come to accept that our brains are flawed and biased, that our politics are tribal and unscientific, and that reality itself is so subjective that we pick and choose what to believe when consuming the news and sharing our views on social media. But this is usually where the conversation with the reader ends. We are too often left wondering, *So what do we do about it?!*

You hold in your hands a book's worth of answers. Gleb Tsipursky, PhD, has created something that, shockingly, is rare in the space we set aside for discussing cognitive biases—a plan for "debiasing" ourselves and our institutions. Throughout this text, Tsipursky shows we are now coming into an age in which scientists are no longer waving their hands at our biased brains nor resigning themselves to melancholy over our forever-irrational ways. There's a new wave of thinking about to hit bookshelves and airports, books like the one, in which scientists and science communicators are optimistic, hopeful, and helpful.

Yes, it's true that you can't delete confirmation bias from your brain when perusing headlines, nor can you prevent yourself from making the fundamental attribution error when someone cuts you off in traffic, nor from falling into the spell of the halo effect when meeting people with impressive mustaches or especially shiny shoes—but in this book, you will learn how to train yourself to turn off your intuitive autopilot so you can pause, reflect, ponder, and predict your way to better decisions, healthier relationships, and a more reasonable appreciation for footwear and facial hair.

We have entered an era where is it more crucial than ever to understand the natural, normal, baked-in mental stumbling blocks each of us shares with our fellow human beings. We need that understanding so we can work to create institutions, governments, and private lives that take them into account instead of stubbornly pretending we are always careful, logical, and rational. As you will learn in the pages that follow, for each cognitive bias discovered so far, there exists a strategy for avoiding the damage it can cause. We can develop game plans and exercises, checklists and best practices, and we can add all this to a new, shared instruction manual for operating our minds.

Why does this feel so new and exciting? Why hasn't this book already been written? Well, the research in this domain is new and the findings fresh. Naturally, the first books on these topics merely explained what we knew so far. So, beyond cataloging our strange thoughts, beliefs, and behaviors, we haven't been offered much in the way of strategy for dealing with them. My own work has contributed to this. Since the turn of the millennium, I've been telling anyone who would listen that while it is true that we humans are capable of reason and rationality, of skepticism and measured responses to complex problems, we often fall short of those ideals, and when we do fall short, we often fail to notice, and we proceed with a sort of undeserved confidence in our past performances. In other words: we are biased, but we don't know it, so keep that in mind before you make a decision that will lead to debt, regret, and stomach upset.

I can think of no better person than Gleb Tsipursky to move the conversation forward. Not only is he a professor of behavioral science, his job title is literally disaster avoidance expert, and after twenty years of working with organizations to avoid the problems that arise when humans try to make sense of reality in groups, he has produced a slew of books and articles and lectures based on his experience. He is devoted to exploring the sort of disasters that he knows are avoidable once you apply the scientific method to self-sabotage. In this book, that's exactly what he does. With each chapter, he reveals that we can do more than just explain what is happening in our heads when we fall prey to bias. We can actively, purposefully, and meaningfully *de*bias ourselves in the situations that matter to us most: our relationships with others.

Please, turn the page and take Gleb's hand into a new era of writing about the psychology of reasoning, one in which you can easily rearrange your life in all sorts of ways to avoid stumbling over your own brain. With his help, you'll see how to keep cognitive biases from making a mess of things in your life, your job, and the institutions and communities you care about most.

—David McRaney, May 2019

Introduction

Please look behind you. No seriously, turn your neck and look behind you.

What did you feel when you did that? Probably some discomfort in your neck, right? What did you see? Unless you have owl heritage, you couldn't turn your neck 180 degrees, and so your field of vision behind you was incomplete.

We learned the simple motion of twisting our necks to look behind us during our childhood to address the visual blindspots we all have. These blindspots behind our backs were obvious to us, posing a clear danger if we didn't address them.

You probably don't even remember how you learned to twist your neck to protect yourself from those blindspots. However, you might remember better learning to address blindspots when you drive. Remember how your driving instructor taught you to not rely only on the car mirrors when changing lanes, but to make sure to peek over your shoulder to address the mirror's blindspot? Unlike the blindspots behind our backs, these blindspots of our car mirrors are not at all obvious. However, failing to address them is very dangerous. I might not be here to write these words if I didn't learn to defend myself from these blindspots following the directions of the driving instructor: I recall avoiding several near disasters on the highway by taking a quick glance before changing lanes.

Unfortunately, we also have hidden blindspots in our minds that often ruin our relationships and other areas of our lives. Yet there are no driving instructors to teach us to watch out for these unconscious mental blindspots, what scholars term "cognitive biases." Why is no one helping us watch out for the devastating consequences of these dangerous judgment errors? Because the research on the nature and dangers of these mental blindspots is relatively new and scholars in psychology, behavioral economics, cognitive neuroscience, and related fields are still finding more and more cognitive biases every year: so far, over one hundred have been found, and with additional information emerging, the field of discovery is not yet settled. Even more cutting-edge scholarship has emerged in the last few years in "debiasing"—the practice of reducing or eliminating cognitive biases—permitting us to gain many new techniques to address these mental blindspots.

Yet as I see it, it's immoral to wait for the many decades it usually takes for the field to settle sufficiently for the science to percolate into public consciousness through public education. People are suffering disasters daily because they fall into cognitive biases. The resulting misconceptions, misunderstandings, and mistakes result in severely damaged or completely broken relationships with their romantic partners, friends, families, and work colleagues, as well as within community groups and civic and political engagements. Cognitive biases also undermine our society as a whole. Some of the worst excesses of polarization and hatred stem from the consequences of failing to watch out for and address these blindspots between us.

Tragically, traditional relationship advice on how to deal with others in all areas of our lives—personal, professional, civic—suggests that you should "go with your gut." Surely you heard this advice often, as well as some variations of that phrase, such as "trust your instincts" or "be authentic" or "follow your intuition." Yet such advice doesn't account for the latest research on how our brain is wired and the mistakes we make as a result of problems with our brain's basic wiring. I'm deeply frustrated, saddened, and angered when I see great relationships ruined because someone bought into the toxic advice of going with their gut. Perhaps they returned home from a Tony Robbins seminar and started to follow their instincts and behave like their "authentic selves," shooting themselves—and their relationships—in the foot. Such advice is meant to make you feel good and appeal to your instincts and intuitions, which is why people embrace it, and why gurus like Robbins get paid megabucks to dispense it. As marketers say, "You can't go wrong telling people what they want to hear," and people want to hear what's comfortable for them. Regrettably, our gut reactions are adapted for the ancient savanna, not the modern world. Following our intuition leads to terrible decisions in the modern environment. For the sake of our relationships, we need to avoid following our primitive instincts and instead be civilized about how we address the inherently flawed nature of our minds.

Thus, I've written the first book focusing on cognitive biases in relationships. Now, you might have read something about these mental blindspots and how they cause us to be screwed up. This book definitely goes in-depth into the problems caused by cognitive biases. However, unlike the vast majority of writings on cognitive biases, its true pay-off is in solving these dangerous judgment errors by drawing on the very latest groundbreaking research in the science on debiasing to help you build better relationships.

As a scholar of behavioral science, and coach and consultant for business and nonprofit leaders, I have been using this research to help my clients—and myself—avert relationship disasters. My deep passion about this topic is personal. Here's why.

As a kid, my dad told me with utmost conviction and absolutely no reservation to "go with your gut." I ended up making some really bad decisions in my relationships that resulted in losing friends and business colleagues. I also watched him make some terrible choices that gravely harmed my family as he followed his gut and fell into cognitive biases, such as hiding some of his salary from my mom for several years. After she discovered this and several other financial secrets he kept, her trust in him was broken, which was one of the major factors leading to their later prolonged separation; fortunately, they eventually reconciled, but the lack of trust can never be fully repaired.

My conviction that the omnipresent advice to "follow your gut" was hollow grew only stronger as I came of age during the dotcom boom and bust and the fraudulent accounting scandals around the turn of the millennium. Seeing prominent business leaders blow through hundreds of millions in online-based businesses without effective revenue streams—Webvan, Boo.com, Pets.com—was sobering, especially as I saw the hype that convinced investors to follow their intuition and put all this money into dotcoms. Likewise, it seemed almost unreal to learn at around the same time about how the top executives of Enron, Tyco, and WorldCom used illegal accounting practices to scam investors. Since their crimes would inevitably be discovered, leading to ruined reputations and long jail sentences, the best explanation for their seemingly irrational behavior comes from their willingness to follow their guts. It was depressing for me to read the accounts of employees, stockholders, and communities devastated by the bankruptcies, especially in cases such as Enron, where the corporate leaders encouraged their employees to buy stocks while themselves selling stock as the company danced on the brink of disaster.

As someone with an ethical code of utilitarianism—desiring the most good for the most number—I felt a calling to reduce suffering and improve well-being by learning about how and why people make the choices that they do and how to improve their decisions. Therefore, I pursued a doctorate focused on decision making in historical settings at the University of North Carolina at Chapel Hill, and later taught as a tenure-track professor in Ohio State University's Decision Sciences Collaborative and History Department, publishing dozens of peer-reviewed papers in venues such as *Behavior and Social Issues*, *Journal of Social and Political Psychology*, and *International Journal of Existential Psychology and Psychotherapy*.

I discovered how the decisions we make are intricately tied to our cognitive biases, which is why the typical "go with your gut" advice usually harms rather than helps our lives and relationships. Driven by my utilitarian value set to be passionate about reducing suffering and improving well-being not only for my students, but for all people—and motivated by the example both of my mom and dad as well as the dot-com boom and bust and the accounting corruption scandals—I started to speak and write about decision making outside of academia, reaching a broad audience. Eventually, I shifted away from academia to devote my full-time efforts to consulting, coaching, speaking, and writing as the CEO of the boutique consulting and training firm Disaster Avoidance Experts (http://disasteravoidanceexperts.com). The organization focuses on helping mid-size and large businesses and nonprofits improve collaboration and teamwork, cultivate employee engagement and motivation, and resolve persistent people problems: in other words, relationship issues. My paradigm-shifting content was featured in over 400 articles I wrote and over 350 interviews I gave to popular venues that include *Fast Company*, *CBS News*, *Time*, *Scientific American*, *Psychology Today*, *The Conversation*, *Business Insider*, *Government Executive*, *Inc. Magazine*, and *CNBC*, and you might have learned about this book from one of them.

If you like the style of one or more of those mainstream venues, you will like the engaging and absorbing style of this book. Please note that the book is meant to be read in the order in which it is written, as each chapter builds upon the previous one. Concepts mentioned in earlier chapters will not be explained in later ones, so I strongly recommend that you read this book from beginning to end rather than dipping in at various points.

You will see me say this several times throughout the book: I *very strongly* recommend that you do the exercises in the book when you encounter them. No, I'm serious. Really. That's why I italicized *very strongly*.

The exercises are not an afterthought, a take-it-or-leave-it part of the book. The research on debiasing cognitive biases shows that simply learning about these mental blindspots is not effective for preventing them. Instead, we need to identify (1) where these dangerous judgment errors might be playing a role in our relationships; (2) how cognitive biases harmed us in the past, are harming us now, and might harm us in the future; and (3) a specific plan to address these mental blindspots. The exercises are meant to achieve all three goals. I'll repeat this because many of you won't believe me at first: just breezing through the book will not do it for you. Please don't make the mistake of skipping the exercises, as I really would hate for you to suffer the damaging consequences of doing so. Additional resources from the book are available on the book's website: http://disasteravoidanceexperts. com/blindspots.

So let's go on to help you protect yourself and your relationships from mental blindspots. In the first chapter, we'll explore recent findings on the structure of our brain and why we have cognitive biases as well as the research on effective techniques to address these biases.

Autopilot vs. Intentional

We are usually advised to go with our gut and trust our intuition, especially in our relationships. And we tend to follow this advice.

We determine our romantic partners by our gut feelings, believing that "the one" will cause us to experience butterflies in our stomach. We pick friends based on our intuitions, choosing the ones with whom we click instantly and have easy and comfortable conversations. We decide which business partners to work with or whom to hire by evaluating our gut reactions about whether we feel intuitively like the person deserves our trust. We choose our churches or secular groups, and other forms of community belonging, by what our intuitions tell us about others in that community. We determine who deserves our votes and campaign contributions through considering how we feel about the political candidates in each race, such as through the famous "beer test": With which candidate would you rather have a beer?

Sadly, just going with our gut frequently leads to devastating results for our relationships. It's an often-cited statistic that over 40 percent of marriages end up in divorce.[1] Trusting our intuition by going with the person who makes us experience that fluttery sensation upon first meeting is a major contributor to this terribly high rate since studies show that our first impressions are often wrong.[2] We have many unnecessary fights with friends that lead to hurt feelings and friendship breakups due to miscommunications and misunderstandings resulting from gut responses to what our friends shared.

Business relationships suffer and discriminatory hiring predominates when we let our guts lead. As an example, a study demonstrated that a recruiter showing stronger negative implicit associations with Arab-Muslim men decreases the likelihood of the recruiter offering interviews to Arab-Muslim job applicants.[3] Another study showed that employers who showed excessive risk aversion were less likely to hire gay men.[4] Let's not even speak of what happens when voters choose the folks they would rather have a beer with over ones who would formulate the best policy for our country.[5]

These problems result from systematic and predictably dangerous judgment errors we tend to make in our relationships, as well as other life areas, which behavioral science scholars term "cognitive biases."[6] This chapter explains cognitive biases and provides some overarching strategies for how to deal with them effectively. The following chapters offer insights on specific cognitive biases, how they impact our relationships, and how we can protect our relationships from these dangerous judgment errors.

How Our Gut Reactions Hurt Our Relationships

The scope of this problem became crystal clear to me in graduate school when I was beginning to study the kinds of errors we human beings make when we simply trust our gut. At the time, I was doing some teaching as a graduate student. At the end of my first semester of teaching, my supervisor called me into his office and gave me some constructive criticism about my performance.

He was somewhat rough and forceful in his delivery of the criticism. Perhaps he didn't need to use the term "lily-livered coward" when describing what he perceived as the excessively high scores I gave my students. Naturally, I felt very grateful for his advice and thanked him immediately and profusely…NOT! What I really wanted to do was shout back at him, tell him he was wrong, and say that his grading system sucked. That's what my gut was telling me to do. My face turned bright red, and I clenched my fists: my gut was also telling me to pop him one.

It took everything I had to restrain myself, dial down my emotions, and stop myself from yelling back or doing something even worse. I wouldn't have had much of a career in academia—or anywhere—if I couldn't do it. Through a haze of red, I told him I'd do what he wanted with the grading system and slunk out of his office with a scowl on my face and my fists clenching and unclenching. I ended up changing my grading style to suit his preferences—he was my boss, after all, and I wanted the teaching gig.

Were you ever in a situation when you received constructive criticism—well-delivered or rough—from your boss, your customer, your spouse, or your friend? What did your gut tell you to do in that moment? Did it tell you to be aggressive and shout back? Perhaps it told you to hunker down and disengage? Maybe it pushed you to put your fingers in your ears with a "la-la-la, I can't hear you."

Behavioral scientists call these three types of responses the "fight, freeze, or flight" response. You might have heard about it as the saber-tooth tiger response, meaning the system in our brain that evolved to deal with threats in our ancestral savanna environment. Our gut prepares us to deal with a serious threat, whether by fighting off an invading tribe, fleeing an avalanche, or freezing and hoping the saber-tooth tiger doesn't notice us.

These responses stem from the older parts of our brain, such as the amygdala, which developed early in our evolutionary process. Our bodies are flooded by the stress hormones cortisol and adrenaline, which boost energy and heart rate to prepare us for dealing effectively with physical threats, while decreasing blood flow to our brain, which impairs wise decision making.

Systems of Thinking (and Feeling)

Fight, freeze, or flight forms a central part of one of the two systems of thinking and feeling that, roughly speaking, determine our mental processes. It's not the old Freudian model of the id, the ego, and the super-ego, which has been left behind by recent research.[7] One of the main scholars in this field is Daniel Kahneman, who won the Nobel Prize for his research on behavioral economics. He calls the two systems of thinking System 1 and System 2, but I think "autopilot system" and "intentional system" describe these systems more clearly.[8]

The autopilot system corresponds to our emotions and intuitions—that's where we get the fight, freeze, or flight response, along with all other instant reactions. This system guides our daily habits, helps us make snap decisions, and reacts instantly to daily life situations, whether dangerous or not. While helping our survival in the past, the fight, freeze, or flight response is not a great fit for many aspects of modern life. We have many small stresses that are not life-threatening, but the autopilot system treats them as saber-tooth tigers, producing an unnecessarily stressful everyday life experience that undermines our mental and physical well-being.

Moreover, the snap judgments resulting from intuitions and emotions usually feel "true" precisely because they are fast and powerful. In fact, the decisions arising from our gut reactions are often right when we are in a situation that matches the ancestral savanna environment well.[9]

For example, you don't want to wait and ponder about whether you should jump out of the way of baseball that looks like it might hit your head. Maybe it will miss, maybe not; ducking won't hurt either way. Similarly, following an impulse to help a drowning child—which helped the whole tribe survive in the savanna— will also generally serve you (and others) well in the modern world. In emergencies, the instinct to listen to those who display savanna-like signs of authority, such as a commanding voice and authoritative gestures, is probably a good idea.

Unfortunately, in too many cases, the snap judgments are wrong. The autopilot system frequently leads us astray, in systematic and predictable ways, in situations that don't match the savanna environment. To protect our relationships, these situations require a greater reliance on the intentional system.

The intentional system reflects rational thinking and centers around the prefrontal cortex, the part of the brain that evolved more recently. According to recent research, it developed as humans started to live within larger social groups. This thinking system helps us handle more complex mental activities, such as managing individual and group relationships, logical reasoning, probabilistic thinking, and learning new information and patterns of thinking and behavior. While the automatic system requires no conscious effort to function, the intentional system requires a deliberate effort to turn on and is mentally tiring. Fortunately, with enough motivation and appropriate training, the intentional system can turn on in situations where the autopilot system is prone to make systematic and predictable errors— cognitive biases. Here's a quick visual comparison of the two systems:

Autopilot System	Intentional System
Fast, intuitive, emotional	Conscious, reasoning, mindful
Requires no effort	Takes intentional effort to turn on and drains mental energy
Automatic thinking, feeling, and behavior habits	Used mainly when we learn new information and use reason and logic
Mostly makes good decisions, but is prone to some predictable and systematic errors	Can be trained to turn on when it detects the autopilot system making errors

We tend to think of ourselves as rational thinkers, usually using the intentional system. Unfortunately, that's not the case.

The autopilot system has been compared by scholars to an elephant. It's by far the more powerful and predominant of the two systems. Our emotions can often overwhelm our rationality. Moreover, our intuition and habits dominate the majority of our life—we're usually in autopilot mode. Yet that's not a bad thing at all—it would be mentally exhausting to think intentionally about our every action and decision.

The intentional system is like the elephant's rider. It can guide the elephant deliberately to go in a direction that matches our actual goals.[10]

Certainly, the elephant part of the brain is huge and unwieldy, slow to turn and change, and stampeding at threats. At the same time, an important strength of the elephant part of our brain involves enabling us to cover a lot of ground at once, something that the rider couldn't do if just walking. Imagine if you had to think thoroughly about everything you do: you'd need a nap right after breakfast!

Fortunately, we can train the elephant. Your rider can become an elephant whisperer. Over time, you can use the intentional system to change your automatic thinking, feeling, and behavior patterns and become a better agent at achieving your goals.[11]

Want to see what the tension between the autopilot system and the intentional system feels like in real life? Think back to the last party you went to that had a nice dessert spread. How hard was it to resist taking that second cookie? That resistance is the intentional system using its limited resources—what we term willpower—to override the gut reaction cravings of the autopilot system.[12]

In the savanna environment, we needed to eat as much sugar as possible. That evolutionary impulse is still with us in the modern world, despite the overabundance of sugary confections. Simply knowing about it is unfortunately insufficient protection: cheesecake is my Achilles heel.

For another example, consider the last flame war you got into online or perhaps an in-person argument with your loved one. Did the flame war or in-person argument solve things? Did you manage to convince the other person? I'd be surprised to learn that it did. Arguments usually don't lead to anything beneficial: often, even if we win the argument, we end up harming relationships we care about. It's like cutting off your nose to spite your face: a bad idea all around.

Looking back, you probably regret at least some of the flame wars or in-person arguments in which you've engaged. If so, why did you engage? It's the old fight response coming to the fore without you noticing it. Unlike that situation with my boss, it's not immediately obvious that a fight response will hurt you down the road. Thus, you let the elephant go rogue, and it stampeded all over the place. In relationships, letting loose the elephant is like allowing a bull into a china shop: broken dishes will be the least of your problems.[13]

Sure, in some cases gut reactions can be helpful in relationship decision-making contexts; in other words, it's not necessarily a bad idea to follow your gut. For instance, a great deal of experience on a topic where you get quick and accurate feedback on your judgments may enable your intuition to pick up valuable and subtle signals that more objective measurements may not discern. Our intuition is good at learning patterns, and immediate feedback about our decision making helps us develop high-quality expertise through improving pattern recognition. Thus, if you spend a great deal of time with a friend, you will likely learn how to read their signals, and your intuition will be well calibrated to respond quickly to them. Your friendship is reflective of how we lived in the savanna environment, namely in tribes, where we had to rely on our gut reactions to evaluate fellow tribal members.

However, don't buy into the myth that you can tell apart lies from truths: studies show that we—yes, that means you too unless you're a trained CIA interrogator—are very bad at distinguishing falsehoods from accurate statements. In fact, research by Charles Bond Jr. and Bella DePaulo shows that on average we detect only 54 percent of lies, a shocking statistic considering we'd get 50 percent if we used random chance.[14]

Overall, it's never a good idea to just go with your gut. Even in cases where you think you can rely on your intuition, it's best to use your instincts as just a warning sign of potential danger and evaluate the situation analytically. For example, your friend might have just gotten some bad news about their family, and their demeanor caused your instincts to misread the situation. Your extensive experience with a given relationship might bring you to ruin if the context changes without you knowing it and you find yourself using your old intuition in a different environment, like a fish out of water.

The example with the cookie is an instance where the tension between the autopilot and the intentional system was obvious.

Online flame wars and in-person arguments are instances where the tension is less obvious but still clearly there. Scholars use the term "akrasia" to refer to a situation where we act against our better judgment.[15] In other words, we act irrationally, defined in behavioral science as going against our own self-reflective goals.

It's really hard to recognize when we engage in akrasia, partly because even realizing that we have two separate mental systems is counterintuitive, not aligning with our self-perception. Our mind feels like a cohesive whole, not like separate intentional and autopilot systems, with each having many complex subsystems.

Take a (mental) step back and observe what happens when you read the following: the last word of this sentence is *underlined.*

Why did that feel uncomfortable? Because you were processing what you saw both using your intentional and your autopilot system. When we read, we rely mostly on the autopilot system for recognizing the words. By making the false statement about underlining, I turned on your intentional system, since what you read did not match what you saw.

That simple example is one of many where you can recognize that what happens in your brain is not simply the rider. We can only perceive consciously the intentional parts of ourselves, and because that's what we see, we think that's all there is. That false self-perception results from our inability to reach within ourselves and grasp the truth about ourselves, namely that the conscious, self-reflective part of us is like a little rider on top of that huge elephant of emotions and intuitions.

There is no actual "there" there: our sense of self is a construct that results from multiple complex and competing mental processes within the autopilot and intentional system. The self-perception of cohesiveness is simply a comfortable myth that helps us make it through the day. When I first found that out, it blew my mind. It takes a bit of time to incorporate this realization into your mental model of yourself and others, in other words how you perceive your mind to work.

Your Cognition Is Biased

As you might have already guessed, many of the systematic and predictable judgment errors we make—cognitive biases—come from our evolutionary heritage. Certain judgment errors helped us survive in the savanna environment, such as overreacting to the presence of a perceived threat. It proved more helpful for our survival to jump at a hundred shadows than fail to jump at one poisonous snake: we are the descendants of those people evolutionarily selected for jumping at shadows. Of course, most cognitive biases do not serve us well in our modern environment, just like mental habits we learned as children may well not serve us well as adults.[16]

Other reasons for cognitive biases result from inherent limitations in our mental processing capacities, such as our difficulty keeping track of many varied data points. That's why simple formulas often outperform experts.

Most cognitive biases result from mistakes made by going with our gut reactions, meaning autopilot system errors. More rarely, cognitive biases are associated with intentional system errors. As you can see in the argument example above: you may have used reason and logic to win the argument, but in the end, you behaved irrationally by harming yourself if cultivating the relationship was more important to you than winning the argument.

Research has identified more than one hundred cognitive biases that cause us to make terrible decisions and destroy our relationships. Broadly speaking, cognitive biases fall into four broad categories: inaccurate evaluations of oneself, of others, of risks and rewards, and of resources. This book will mainly focus on evaluations of others, which is the category most responsible for damaging relationships.

Throughout the book, I'll give tentative evolutionary explanations for a number of biases, reflecting plausible scenarios for how they might have resulted from our evolutionary heritage based on my reading of the current scientific literature. It's quite possible that these explanations will be updated and changed by newer findings while far from all scholars will fully agree with my interpretations. That's what it means to read research that's on the cutting edge, instead of staid textbooks that contain research a generation or two out-of-date.

So that's bad news, right? Our minds are messed up. We're screwed. End of play, curtain down, you can go home now.

But wait, there's more! Not all hope is lost. Our intentional system can be trained to spot situations where we're likely to make mistakes due to cognitive biases and correct these errors.

I'm not saying it's easy as doing so involves building up many mental habits that you don't have now. If you want easy, you can put this book down right now and go watch some TV to make sure you keep up with the Kardashians.

If you want to have great relationships in real life, you'll need to put in some effort. No pain, no gain, right? Developing the mental habits described in this book is like going to gym for your mind. I'd say it's much more important than that though. What can be more important than improving your relationships—in all life areas? Our lives are determined by our social web of interactions with others, and if you screw up your relationships, don't expect that you'll have the kind of life you want.

Not what you hoped to hear? Here's something more hopeful. You'll be cheered by the fact that the strategies outlined below all come from research in psychology, behavioral economics, cognitive neuroscience, and other disciplines that investigate how to debias cognitive biases.[17] Debiasing is the practice of addressing the cognitive biases that lead to devastating consequences as a result of our decision making, in relationships and other areas.[18] Along with discussing debiasing methods, the rest of the book will also lay out tactics informed by cognitive behavioral therapy for integrating these approaches into your everyday activities, to help you build up the mental habits needed to protect your relationships.

These Are Not Cognitive Biases

Before talking about solving cognitive biases, it helps to clarify some common areas of confusion around these dangerous judgment errors. As used in the scholarly literature, and in this book, the term "cognitive bias" differs from other ways you might have heard "bias" term used, such as social biases relating to discrimination and stereotyping based on race, gender, sexuality, ethnicity, ability, age, and so on.

A cognitive bias is a predictable pattern of mental errors that results in misperceiving reality and, as a result, deviates from reaching goals, whether in relationships or other life areas. In other words, from the perspective of what is best for us as individuals, falling for a cognitive bias always harms us by lowering the probability of getting what we want. Some cognitive biases result in social biases, when they cause us to have an excessively positive or negative view of people based on gender, sexuality, ethnicity, and other characteristics.

Yet, despite cognitive biases sometimes leading to discriminatory thinking and feeling patterns, these are two separate and distinct concepts. Cognitive biases are common across humankind and relate to the particular wiring of our brains, while social biases relate to perceptions between different groups and are specific for the society in which we live. For example, I bet you don't care or even think about whether someone is a noble or a commoner, yet that distinction was fundamentally important a few centuries ago across Europe. To take another example—a geographic instead of one across time—most readers of this book probably don't have strong feelings about Sunni versus Shiite Muslims, yet this distinction is incredibly meaningful in many parts of the world.

Neither are cognitive biases the same thing as cognitive distortions. The concept of "cognitive distortions" is a tool within CBT aimed at addressing depression and anxiety.[19] Therapists use the term "cognitive distortions" to describe a variety of irrational thinking patterns that lead to negative moods, with the goal of helping individuals notice and challenge such thinking patterns.

Cognitive biases are a different beast. These errors have to do with judgment, not mood. Ironically, cognitive biases can lead to positive moods, such as the optimism bias and overconfidence effect. Of course, the consequence of falling into cognitive biases, once discovered, usually leaves us in a bad mood due to the disastrous results of these dangerous judgment errors. In some cases, cognitive biases might contribute to cognitive distortions. A case in point, the pessimism bias may contribute to the cognitive distortion known as catastrophizing, which is when we exaggerate small problems into huge catastrophes, leading to anxious and depressive moods. However, cognitive biases and cognitive distortions are two separate things.

Finally, cognitive biases differ from logical fallacies. Logical fallacies are errors in reasoning that people make during disagreements, usually with the intention of using underhanded strategies to win an argument. One common one is called "cherry-picking," which is when someone selects a small sample of evidence that supports their side of an argument out of a much larger pool of evidence, some of which opposes their perspective. By contrast, cognitive biases are errors we all tend to make in our own judgments, rather than manipulative tactics to win an argument.

Now, cognitive biases make us vulnerable to manipulation by logical fallacies. For example, with the cognitive bias known as attentional bias, our tendency to pay attention to the most emotionally salient features of our environment, contributes to our frequent failure to notice the vast amount of evidence available from which an underhanded debater cherry-picks their points. One of the side benefits of studying cognitive biases is that doing so helps us avoid being manipulated by advertisers, politicians, and other skilled manipulators.

Debiasing Cognitive Biases

Now, without further ado, let's get to the specific methods involved in debiasing. A great deal of debiasing involves some form of shifting from the autopilot to the intentional mode of thinking.

Identifying Our Cognitive Biases and Making Plans to Address Them

First of all, we need to learn about the various cognitive biases that we might be facing, especially the ones to which we are most vulnerable due to our individual personality and upbringing. Sounds obvious, right? Awareness of the problem is the first step to solving the problem. However, effective debiasing through education about cognitive biases is trickier than it might seem. Wouldn't it be wonderful if you could just read a book or listen to a lecture about a cognitive bias, and voila, you're cured!

Unfortunately, it's not that easy. Research suggests that just knowing about a cognitive bias frequently doesn't solve this problem.[20] Much more effective education methods involve evaluating where in our life this mental error tends to lead us astray and to cause pain and then making a specific plan to address the problem.

Most likely this method is effective because addressing the autopilot system requires inspiring strong emotions. Changing our habitual instincts is hard, and I mean *hard*. We have to really want to do it, meaning we have to invest strong emotions because we really dislike the current situation. To make that investment, it's critical for us to have personal buy-in for transforming our intuition. Simply learning about the cognitive bias doesn't create the necessary intense feelings. However, identifying in a deep and thorough manner where that dangerous judgment error is truly hurting us as individuals and our relationships—the critical pain points in our personal, professional, and civic lives—helps empower the strong negative emotions needed to go against our gut reactions.[21]

Yet even that is not enough, just like it wouldn't be enough to dislike strongly our body weight without a tangible plan to get fit through changing our diet and exercise regimen. And make no mistake, the work you're about to do to become mentally fit is just as hard as the work required to make a drastic change for the better in your physical health.

To help you achieve your mental fitness goals, this book has exercises for you to do in each chapter where you will self-reflect on where each cognitive bias causes you problems in your life and how you plan to fix the issues caused by the bias. Reading the book without doing the exercise is like leaping half-way across a deep hole: you'll end up worse than you started. Reading this book without doing the work would have just as much impact on addressing the blindspots as would reading a book on diet and exercise without taking the steps described in that book. In both cases, you'll be much more aware of the problems without solving them and end up suffering more than you would if you remained in blissful ignorance. I don't recommend it, and the Kardashians await if that's what you want to do.

Still here? Good. Please do yourself and those you care about the favor of doing the exercises to help protect and improve your relationships.

Delaying Our Decisions and Reactions

One of the simplest ways to shift from the autopilot to the intentional mode of thinking involves *delaying our decisions and reactions*. Remember when your mom told you to count to ten when you're angry? Well, it works!

So do other similar techniques to stop yourself from reacting on autopilot, such as a mindful pause before responding to a negative external stimulus. Instead, give yourself the time and space needed to cool down and make a more reasoned, slower response to the situation.[22]

While counting to ten works for an immediate response situation—our intentional system takes a second or two to turn on, while the autopilot system takes only milliseconds—a more intense arousal response will require about *twenty to thirty minutes* to calm down. That length of time is how long it takes our *sympathetic nervous system*, which is the system activated in fight, freeze, and flight responses, to cool down through turning on our *parasympathetic nervous system*, also called the rest-and-digest system.

Probabilistic Thinking

Our autopilot system does not do well with numbers: it's in essence a "yes" or "no" system, attraction or aversion, threat or opportunity. This type of thinking can be solved through the intentional system approach of applying *probabilistic thinking* to evaluate reality.[23] Also called *Bayesian reasoning*, after the creator of the Bayesian Theorem, Rev. Thomas Bayes, probabilistic thinking involves evaluating the probability of what reality looks

like and updating your beliefs about the world as more information becomes available.[24]

For instance, say your spouse said something hurtful and your
intuitive response is to say something mean in response. A probabilistic thinking approach involves stepping back and evaluating
the likelihood that your spouse meant to hurt you or whether a
miscommunication occurred. You would then seek further evidence to help you update your beliefs about whether your spouse
meant to hurt you or not.[25]

As an example, if she says, "Wow, our electric bill is so high
this month," and you like the house to be warm in the winter and
set the thermostat high, it's easy to feel the comment to be an
attack on you and say something hurtful in response. For instance,
if she has been unemployed for a while and hasn't been successful
in finding a job, a hurtful (and all-too-typical) response would be,
"Well, we wouldn't have to worry about the size of the bill if we
had more money coming in." Drama follows.

By contrast, probabilistic thinking would cause you to evaluate the likelihood of her seeking to hurt you and seek more evidence first before deciding how to respond. Thus, you might ask,
"Are you concerned about the electricity costs of me setting the
thermostat high?" Then, she can respond, for instance, saying,
"Well, the electric bill is about two times as high as last month,
and you were running the thermostat then. I think the electric
company just screwed up. I'll call them tomorrow." Domestic conflict averted, thanks to probabilistic thinking (I had a version of
this conversation with my wife last winter).

A key aspect of probabilistic thinking consists of using your
existing knowledge about the likely shape of reality (called the
"base rate probability," also known as "prior probability") to evaluate new evidence. In a keynote for a group of Fifth Third Bank
managers on using debiasing techniques to improve organizational performance, I spoke about using base rates to determine

how to invest time and energy into mentoring subordinates most effectively. In a facilitated exercise, I asked them to consider how their prior mentoring impacted their subordinates. Then, I asked them to compare the qualities of their current subordinates to the prior subordinates they mentored. Finally, I asked them to consider whether their mentoring energy was invested effectively compared to the impact they could have on subordinates.

"Base rates" here refers to their prior experience of investing energy into mentoring and the kind of outcomes they achieved. The discussion revealed that the current behavior of bank managers did not match their estimates of employee improvement. In fact, the managers were overall spending way too much time mentoring the worst performers, perhaps 70 percent of their time on average, whereas the biggest impact of mentoring based on their prior experience came from improving the performance of their best performers. Informed by this evaluation of prior probabilities and how they compared to current actions, the managers determined to shift their mentoring energies and recommend that the worst performers get an outside coach, even if doing so would negatively impact their relationship to these employees.

Making Predictions About the Future

A related strategy involves *making predictions about the future*.[26] Let's say you think your parents will be mad if you and your husband and kids don't visit them for Thanksgiving and that they won't accept your explanation of being really exhausted due to job stress. Write down your prediction and then have a conversation with your parents. See whether your prediction turns out to be true or not. If it doesn't, update your mental model of your parents. In general, updating your mental model of others is crucial to ensuring healthy relationships.

Considering Alternative Explanations

The next debiasing strategy involves *considering alternative explanations*. Say your boss is curt at work. Some people might take this curtness to be a sign that their boss is angry with them. They would start thinking about their past performance, analyzing every aspect of it, and psyching themselves out in a spiral of catastrophizing thinking.

Debiasing in this case involves considering alternative explanations.[27] Perhaps your boss is in a bad mood because her lunch burrito didn't agree with her. Perhaps she's very busy, rushing to fulfill a customer's demands, and didn't have a chance to chat with you as she normally would. Numerous explanations exist for her behavior that do not involve your boss being angry. Combining considering the alternative with probabilistic thinking, you can follow up with your boss later in the day when she seems to have a quiet moment and observe how she interacts with you then, updating your beliefs based on this later interaction.

Considering Our Past Experiences

Considering our past experiences also helps as a debiasing tactic.[28] Do you have trouble with running late to work meetings? Are you the type of person who leaves for a meeting that's fifteen minutes driving distance from you exactly fifteen minutes before the meeting? So what happens when you forget your phone?

Chronic lateness harms your relationships as well as your mental and physical well-being through constant elevated levels of cortisol, the stress hormone. Self-reflecting on how long activities have taken in the past to inform your current activities—for example, exactly when you should start preparing for a meeting to be there with five minutes to spare—will help your relationships and your well-being.

How about the kind of people you end up with in romantic relationships? My relative had a series of boyfriends who emotionally manipulated her. Likely they felt attracted to her because she put out a vibe of being needy and not willing to push back against pressure from these manipulative men.

Her story has a good ending. With the help of a therapist, she looked at her pattern of past experiences of romantic failures. She recognized that her unwillingness to be alone resulted in her excessive willingness to put up with emotional manipulation, including attracting the kind of men likely to do so. By considering her past experience, she recognized a need for herself to grow in her capacity to live alone. She spent some time outside of a romantic relationship—a real hardship for her—and expanded her comfort zone in the ability to live alone.

She then got back onto the dating scene, this time with a much better capacity both to avoid the kind of men likely to manipulate her as well as a full willingness to end any relationships with hints of emotional manipulation. The quality of her relationships improved greatly, all as a result of considering past experiences and improving herself based on past problems.

Reflecting on the Future and Repeating Scenarios

Next, *evaluate the long-term future*—the long-term impact of a major decision or a series of repeating decisions that have a great long-term impact when combined.[29] What happened the last time you asked your spouse to pick up his socks? Did he do what you wanted, or did you see even more socks in the same place a day later? Is this a pattern that repeats again and again until you finally can't stand the sight of his socks and clean them up yourself? If so, why ask him to pick up his socks in the first place? It's not like it will make the situation any better and will only cause more conflict and grief for you both. Maybe it's better to either have a serious conversation with him about picking up his socks or just let it slide. This kind of evaluation of repeating scenarios can greatly improve your social interactions.

Considering Other People's Points of View

You probably heard the saying, "Before you judge a person, walk a mile in their shoes." Turns out this approach—meaning understanding other people's mental models and situation context—is quite helpful for debiasing.[30] We tend to underestimate by a lot the extent to which other people are different than we are. That's why the Golden Rule, "Do unto others as you would have them do unto you," is trumped by what some call the Platinum Rule, "Do unto others as they would like to have done unto them." You'll get much better relationship outcomes if you practice the debiasing strategy of *considering other people's points of view* and focusing on their needs, not simply your own, in your interactions.

Getting an External Perspective

When was the last time you saw two of your friends or family members arguing over something silly? From your outside perspective on the conflict, you recognized that fighting over the issue at hand was not productive and even harmful. Why didn't they see it themselves? Because the inside view—from within a situation—blinds us to the broader context of what's going on, leading to poor decisions that harm our relationships. To help yourself address this problem, get an *external perspective* from someone you trust, which is an excellent debiasing strategy.[31]

Setting a Policy to Guide Your Future Self

One of the easiest ways to address cognitive biases involves *setting a policy that guides our future self.* In the heat of the moment, it may be hard to delay decision making, consider alternatives, or practice the Platinum Rule. Yet if you set a policy by which you abide, especially by using a decision aid, you can protect yourself from many dangerous biases. For example, say you've committed to avoid responding to emails that make you mad for at least thirty minutes. That's a great policy, as it ensures you have enough time to cool down by turning on your parasympathetic nervous system through, say, stepping away from the computer and taking a brief walk outside.

It would work even better with a decision aid, such as Gmail's "undo send" feature. If your elephant gets the better of you and you find yourself typing out an angry response email and sending it, the "undo send" feature allows you to unsend the email, at least for a few seconds after you hit send. Trust me, that feature served me well a number of times (my default response in the saber-tooth scenario is fight). Other decision aides include check-lists or visible reminders that empower us to be our best intentional selves.[32]

Making a Precommitment

A related strategy involves *making a precommitment,* especially a public commitment, to a certain set of behaviors, with an associated accountability mechanism.[33] For instance, pledging to follow a set of ethical guidelines makes us more likely to follow that set of ethics, even when our autopilot system is tempting us to take ethical shortcuts. One pledge I advise everyone reading this book is the Pro-Truth Pledge (see http:/.protruthpledge.org), a public commitment to follow truthful behaviors, which I helped found. Taking this pledge publicly, sharing about it with your social network, and calling on your elected representatives to take it improves the truthfulness of our society, which has been so degraded in recent years.

The public nature of a commitment encourages our community—the people who know about the commitment and care about helping us be our best selves—to support our efforts to change our behavior. Suppose you want to improve your relationships with people by avoiding interrupting them. It would be wise to share that aspiration with those with whom you frequently interact—and whom you frequently interrupt—along with asking them to remind you of your goal and hold you accountable for meeting it. The autopilot system's tendency to cut corners is held in check—at least somewhat—by this commitment.

Practicing Mindfulness Meditation

You won't be surprised that one effective strategy to address cognitive biases involves *mindfulness meditation*. Meditation has been found by research to treat numerous problems, from pain to anxiety; now, we know it also helps us address cognitive biases.[34]

Why? Most likely, due to a combination of delay, awareness, and focus. We are more capable of delaying unhelpful intuitive impulses, being more aware of when we are going with our gut, and focusing more on turning on our intentional system. Now, since mindfulness meditation is an excellent practice that will build up your debiasing ability overall but is not aimed at any cognitive bias in particular, I will only discuss it as a solution in this chapter, so I don't have to repeat it every time. Please keep in mind that it applies to all of the cognitive biases described in this book.

A daily sitting practice of just ten minutes a day will substantially improve your ability to solve all sorts of cognitive biases. Due to the general applicability of mindfulness meditation for debiasing, along with other mental and physical well-being benefits, I cannot stress enough the importance of taking up a daily meditation practice.

For those not familiar with meditation, a breathing practice offers a good place to start. Free up thirty minutes for your first time meditating. Start by sitting in a comfortable position. Then, take in a long breath, counting to five slowly as you breathe in. Hold in your breath for the same five count length, then breathe out while counting to five. Then, wait for another count of five before breathing in again.

Repeat this cycle a couple more times until you grow comfortable with it. Then, at the start of the next cycle when doing the five-count breathing in, focus on the sensations in your nostrils when the air moves past them. Focus fully on that sensation, while still maintaining the pace of slow breathing in. Once you breathe in, keep focusing on your nostrils for the five-count while holding your breath, and notice how they feel different with no air rushing past them. Then, focus once again on air rushing past your nostrils when you breathe out to the count of five, and then once again on the nostrils with no air moving past them while you wait for a five-count before breathing in. Keep doing the five-count breath cycle combined with focusing on your nostrils for the next twenty minutes. Notice whenever your attention wanders away from your nostrils, and bring it back.

That's it—not too hard, right? To build up this practice, first you need to make a personal commitment to freeing up ten minutes a day for doing it. Make sure to do meditation especially when some unexpected emergency occurs. Those are the days when we feel least capable of meditating, yet counterintuitively these are the days when meditation can most help us avoid mistakes and make better decisions.

Then, learn about different approaches to meditation, and experiment with the three major ones: focusing on breathing, focusing on letting go of thoughts (zazen), and focusing on body awareness. You can search for this information online or read books.[35]

After you choose an approach that works best for you, decide on a specific time and place each day when you'll engage in your sitting practice. Consider what reminders you will use to help you remember to pursue this practice, write down your commitment in a journal or email yourself, and share with others in your life about your new mental exercise routine. Be forgiving of yourself if you slip up, and simply get back on the wagon: new habits are notoriously difficult to build. Remember that this mindfulness practice is one of the best things you can do to improve your relationships in all life areas.

Conclusion

The strategies outlined above stem from extensive research on debiasing combined with my own coaching, consulting, and speaking experience. Put simply, they work!

Unlike the vast majority of the relationship advice out there, these strategies are not based simply on what has worked for me. These debiasing tactics work for any human being because we all suffer from dangerous judgment errors that can devastate our relationships. So if you're a human being, you can benefit from this advice (and if you're an alien reading this to learn more about how to conquer the human race, I hope it helps you understand that we will never surrender!).

These strategies have done wonders for my relationships, including during the most difficult relationship experience in my life, when my wife Agnes had what her therapist described as a nervous breakdown in July 2014 due to burnout. She developed debilitating anxiety, combined with periods of occasional depression. Her mental illness was incredibly straining for our relationship.

Any innocent remark from me could drive her to tears. For example, I remember asking her, "Are the dishes clean?" and Agnes just started crying. I had no idea why. We ended up having a five-hour-long conversation that night until 3:00 a.m., figuring out what happened. It turned out that her autopilot system felt pressured and criticized by my question, reading it as implicit disapproval and rejection of her for failing to wash the dishes.

Of course, that was not my intent. Her intentional system recognized it when we discussed the situation calmly, as opposed to her elephant stampeding all over the place in the heat of the moment. That late-night conversation was one of many we had over the next six months since such incidents happened almost daily, and sometimes more than once a day. I don't have words to describe how disconcerting, saddening, and frustrating it was for me to find that the person I knew as my wife was gone, and it was even worse for Agnes. While I remained fully committed to our marriage, both of us knew the situation had to change.

Over time, as a result of implementing a number of debiasing strategies—such as considering alternative explanations for my statements, probabilistic thinking about the reality of dangers versus unrealistic anxious thoughts, and setting a policy to guide our future selves—our relationship got back on track. Setting policies proved especially helpful for shaping our conversations. We resolved not to interact casually during the day, which we used to do regularly, so she did not have to be on constant guard about what was going to happen.

Instead, we learned to interact only in highly structured ways, talking about one topic at a time in a systematic pattern so she could predict and prepare herself for each topic, instead of constantly worrying about what might come up. For example, we started our conversations by checking in about events that happened to us during the day without going in-depth into any topic, especially anything that might require decision making. Next, we would check in about any household matters, and she could prepare herself mentally for discussions about the dishes or any other such topic. Then, we'd discuss any aspects of our day-to-day relationship, such as how we would spend time together in the next week, including putting specific times and dates into our mutual calendar. The rest of the conversation each day flowed in a similar fashion.

Sound awkward? Believe me, it was, especially at first. However, it was not nearly as bad as having Agnes cry at my innocent remarks. These strategies, I firmly believe, saved our marriage. My wife has since mostly recovered, in part thanks to these strategies, and we retain many of them because they help keep our relationship safe. In fact, our relationship is better than it was before we implemented these strategies because we are much more likely to notice any challenges and head them off at the pass.

Let me again emphasize that while these strategies have done wonders for me—in my relationship with my wife and other important relationships in my life—they would also work for anyone else. Not only am I thoroughly convinced by the research on the topic, but also I have seen these debiasing strategies prove very effective for readers of my articles and books, for audience members of my speeches, for the many people I've coached, and for employees in organizations for which I consulted. In the following pages, you will learn about their stories, along with specific cognitive biases and the concrete tactics you can deploy to address these faulty mental patterns by retraining your mind to align with your relationship needs in the modern world. For additional resources from the book, check out the book's website, http://disasteravoidanceexperts.com/blindspots.

Debiasing Strategies Exercises

I promised exercises, and I always keep my promises. For those who think you're going to skip the exercises and come back to them later, please don't. Remember, you're really shooting yourself in the foot if you're not doing these exercises as you're going along with the text of the book. I can cite extensive research telling you that you won't get even a third of the benefit of the book if you don't do the exercises, but do you really want me to spend the ink doing so? You haven't put this book down to catch up with the Kardashians, so just go along a little bit further and get your journal out and get ready to go! Take a few minutes to reflect on the questions below and write down your answers in your journal:

- How can you implement *identifying your cognitive biases and making a plan to address them* to solve cognitive biases in your relationships? Specifically, how will you implement this strategy? What challenges do you anticipate seeing in this implementation, and how will you overcome these challenges? What metrics will you use to measure your success in implementing this approach? What would the future of your relationships look like if you succeed in your implementation?

- How can you implement *delaying decisions and reactions* to solve cognitive biases in your relationships? Specifically, how will you implement this strategy? What challenges do you anticipate seeing in this implementation, and how will you overcome these challenges? What metrics will you use to measure your success in implementing this approach? What would the future of your relationships look like if you succeed in your implementation?

- How can you implement *probabilistic thinking* to solve cognitive biases in your relationships? Specifically, how will you implement this strategy? What challenges do you anticipate seeing in this implementation, and how will you overcome these challenges? What metrics will you use to measure your success in implementing this approach? What would the future of your relationships look like if you succeed in your implementation?

- How can you implement *making predictions about the future* to solve cognitive biases in your relationships? Specifically, how will you implement this strategy? What challenges do you anticipate seeing in this implementation, and how will you overcome these challenges? What metrics will you use to measure your success in implementing this approach? What would the future of your relationships look like if you succeed in your implementation?

- How can you implement *considering alternative explanations* to solve cognitive biases in your relationships? Specifically, how will you implement this strategy? What challenges do you anticipate seeing in this implementation, and how will you overcome these challenges? What metrics will you use to measure your success in implementing this approach? What would the future of your relationships look like if you succeed in your implementation?

- How can you implement *considering past experiences* to solve cognitive biases in your relationships? Specifically, how will you implement this strategy? What challenges do you anticipate seeing in this implementation, and how will you overcome these challenges? What metrics will you use to measure your success in implementing this approach? What would the future of your relationships look like if you succeed in your implementation?

- How can you implement *reflecting on the future and repeating scenarios* to solve cognitive biases in your relationships? Specifically, how will you implement this strategy? What challenges do you anticipate seeing in this implementation, and how will you overcome these challenges? What metrics will you use to measure your success in implementing this approach? What would the future of your relationships look like if you succeed in your implementation?

- How can you implement *considering other people's points of view* to solve cognitive biases in your relationships? Specifically, how will you implement this strategy? What challenges do you anticipate seeing in this implementation, and how will you overcome these challenges? What metrics will you use to measure your success in implementing this approach? What would the future of your relationships look like if you succeed in your implementation?

- How can you implement *getting an external perspective* to solve cognitive biases in your relationships? Specifically, how will you implement this strategy? What challenges do you anticipate seeing in this implementation, and how will you overcome these challenges? What metrics will you use to measure your success in implementing this approach? What would the future of your relationships look like if you succeed in your implementation?

- How can you implement *setting a policy to guide your future self* to solve cognitive biases in your relationships? Specifically, how will you implement this strategy? What challenges do you anticipate seeing in this implementation, and how will you overcome these challenges? What metrics will you use to measure your success in implementing this approach? What would the future of your relationships look like if you succeed in your implementation?

- How can you implement *making a precommitment* to solve cognitive biases in your relationships? Specifically, how will you implement this strategy? What challenges do you anticipate seeing in this implementation, and how will you overcome these challenges? What metrics will you use to measure your success in implementing this approach? What would the future of your relationships look like if you succeed in your implementation?

- How can you implement *mindfulness meditation* to solve cognitive biases in your relationships? Specifically, how will you implement this strategy? What challenges do you anticipate seeing in this implementation, and how will you overcome these challenges? What metrics will you use to measure your success in implementing this approach? What would the future of your relationships look like if you succeed in your implementation?

CHAPTER 2

Our Attribution Errors

Imagine you're driving to the grocery store, thinking about what you're going to buy there. You aren't focusing on all the behaviors needed to drive: instead, your autopilot system is in charge. And that's a good thing. Once you learn how to drive, which takes the extensive deliberate focus of the intentional system, you don't need to use up your mental resources by turning on your intentional system for driving in ordinary driving situations, without inclement weather or start-and-stop traffic. In general, it's wise to let your autopilot system be in charge when you are doing regular, routine, habitual tasks that don't require much focus, whether driving, doing the dishes, or deleting spam emails.

Now imagine that, as you are driving, the car in front of you unexpectedly cuts you off. You slam on your brakes. Maybe you flash your lights or honk your horn. You feel scared and angry: Your sympathetic nervous system activates, shooting cortisol and adrenaline throughout your body. Your heart beats faster; your palms start to sweat; a wave of heat goes through your body.

What's your gut feeling about the other driver? I know my first thought would be that the driver is rude and obnoxious.

Now imagine a different situation: You're driving on autopilot, minding your own business, and you suddenly realize you need to turn right at the next intersection. You quickly switch lanes and suddenly hear someone behind you honking their horn. You now realize that there was someone in your blindspot, but you forgot to check it in the rush to switch lanes, so you cut them off pretty badly.

Do you think that you are a rude driver? The vast majority of us would not. We did not deliberately cut off the other driver; we just failed to see their car.

Finally, imagine a third situation: your friend got hurt, and you're rushing to get your friend to the emergency room. You're driving aggressively and cutting in front of other cars. Are you a rude driver? You'd probably say you are not; you're merely doing the right thing for this situation.

Step back and notice what's going on. These are three different ways of conceptualizing the same event. Let's be honest: we have no idea why the person in the other car cut us off, but we tend to think of them as a jerk, while not seeing ourselves as a jerk in situations where others would ascribe that status to us. Our brains are plagued by a series of attribution errors, the topic of this chapter.

Fundamental Attribution Error

Why do we give ourselves a pass while assigning an obnoxious status to other people? Why does our gut always make ourselves out to be the good guys and other people the bad guys? There is clearly a disconnect between our gut reactions and reality. This pattern is not a coincidence: our immediate gut reaction attributes the behavior of other people to their personality and not to the situation in which the behavior occurs. The scientific name for this type of thinking and feeling is the "fundamental attribution error," also called the "correspondence bias."[36]

This means that if we see someone behaving rudely, we immediately and intuitively feel that this person is rude. We don't stop to consider whether an unusual situation may cause the individual to act that way. With the example of the driver, maybe the person who cut you off did not see you. Maybe they were driving their friend to the emergency room. But that's not what our automatic reaction tells us. On the other hand, we attribute our own behavior to the situation and not our personality. Much of the time we believe that we have valid explanations for our actions.

What explains this erroneous mental pattern? From an evolutionary perspective, in the savanna, it was valuable for our survival to make quick decisions and to assume the worst, regardless of the accuracy of this assumption. In the modern world, where our survival is not immediately threatened by others and where we have long-term interactions with strangers, such judgments are dangerous and harmful, whether about individuals or groups.

Don't believe me that such snap judgments can be harmful? After all, it may not seem very important to your life whether you think wrongly that other drivers are jerks. Sorry to disappoint you, but this mental pattern is very dangerous overall, as the fundamental attribution error can gravely undercut your relationships with others.

As an example, what would you think if you see someone who you just started dating yelling at someone on the phone? You would probably have a negative reaction toward your date and may not be likely to go on another date with that person. Well, what if you found out your date was yelling because her father on the other end had just misplaced his hearing aid, and your date was making plans to go to his house to help him look for it? Or perhaps the date's teenage daughter doesn't take anything seriously unless she's yelled at?

There can be many innocent explanations for someone yelling on the phone, but we are tempted to assume the worst. In another phone-related example, I was coaching a CEO of a company that had many staff who worked from home. He told me about a recent incident with an employee who was having a heated Skype discussion over a conflictual issue with an HR manager. The Skype call disconnected, and the HR manager told the CEO that the employee hung up on her. The CEO fired the employee on the spot. Later, he learned that the employee thought the HR manager hung up on her: the call simply disconnected. Unfortunately, it was too late to take back this firing. This unfair firing situation really demoralized the rest of the staff, and eventually contributed to the CEO leaving the organization.

How about when you see a neighbor leave her trash can on the curb long after a garbage truck picked it up? What do you feel about the neighbor when her garbage can is the only lonely can on the whole block? Isn't it intuitive to feel that the neighbor is just lazy and doesn't care about the appearance of the neighborhood?

I was that neighbor several years ago when my wife Agnes had a nervous breakdown in late 2014. In addition to my full-time professor job and civic commitments, I became her part-time caretaker, spending an additional fifteen to twenty hours and a great deal of emotional and mental energy on this role. It would be an understatement to say that it was an overwhelming experience, and I ended up developing a mental illness myself, an anxiety disorder, which manifested itself mainly as physical fatigue.

While I tried to take care of all the house chores, sometimes I literally had no energy to roll back the trash can for several days. Would you judge me as lazy and uncaring? I hope not, yet such snap judgments based on limited experience and heated emotions are incredibly easy to make. Of course, they would then powerfully shape your relationship to me as a neighbor. Fortunately, our neighbors knew about our situation, since I made sure to go out of my way to inform them. I didn't want them to fall for the fundamental attribution error after all.

For another example from that time period in my life, prior to her nervous breakdown, one of the most important ways Agnes and I spent time together involved taking long hikes in nature preserves, where we combined enjoying each other's company with delighting in nature. One of the reasons we invested our time into this activity is that nature walks have been shown to reduce depression and improve mood.[37] Also, they're just fun! I still recall her pointing out a skunk nonchalantly crossing the road in front of us, and we made sure to stop and give it plenty of room; another time, we waited around to give a male turkey plenty of time to do its mating display to a flock of female turkeys.

Well, after the nervous breakdown, it all ended. Agnes could barely walk downstairs to make breakfast for herself before she had to take a thirty-minute break. She couldn't walk outside at all. Our nature hikes were over. Given the importance of this activity for our relationship, both of us found the situation pretty devastating.

Fundamental Attribution Error Exercise

Before going onward, please STOP! The first step to solving this problem is reflecting on where you might be making such mistakes in your life and where you observe other people making these mistakes. So please take a few minutes to journal your answers to these questions. Don't go onward until you do, otherwise you will lose much of the value of reading this book since research shows that exploring how cognitive biases impact you is fundamentally important to addressing these fallacious mental patterns.

- Where have you fallen into the fundamental attribution error in your life? How has doing so harmed your relationships? Where have you seen other people fall for the fundamental attribution error in their lives? How has doing so harmed their relationships?

Solving the Fundamental Attribution Error

Hey, I see you! You didn't journal your answers to the questions above. Please go back and do so. Don't worry, I can wait. Done? Good. Let's go on.

Delaying our decisions and reactions is a critical debiasing tool for addressing the fundamental attribution error. Snap judgments are notoriously unreliable, and unlike our ancestors on the prehistoric savanna, we modern people don't need to make such judgments for our survival in the vast majority of cases. So when you perceive yourself to be formulating a judgment of someone, notice that you're doing it.

Shift your thought pattern from a set judgment to curiosity. Rather than deciding *what a jerk* after someone behaves in a rude manner, change the self-talk in your internal monologue to, *I wonder if they're a jerk or if it's the circumstances?* Avoid immediately assuming negative things about your date yelling on the phone, and use that curiosity to ask about the situation. Similarly, if you're in a position of power in the office, as was the CEO who fired the employee, make sure to take the time to inquire what happened from everyone involved before making a decision as important as firing someone for cause, which meant no unemployment benefits for the fired employee. In another example, rather than telling yourself, *Well, that's just the type of person they are*, about a behavior you don't like, ask yourself, *Can this person change their behavior, by themselves or with help from someone else?*

For the usefulness of such questioning, it would have been easy for Agnes and I to attribute her inability to walk outside to her new personality. We could have simply accepted the situation and gotten her a wheelchair for when she needed to be outside for me to roll around. Of course, it would have meant we would never be able to take nature hikes and more broadly the end of her self-powered mobility outside the house.

We decided instead to delay judgment on this matter and deliberately try to attribute her inability to walk outside to her circumstances rather than her new personality. In other words, we asked, *Can she change her condition?* Agnes devoted a lot of time to trying to improve her capacity to walk. She began by just sitting outside. Then, she and I sat outside together. Then, she started to walk for a few yards before sitting down. Next, she would take long pauses instead of sitting down. I sometimes joined her in these tiny walks, but most of the time she did these herself.

I'll never forget how, about three months after her nervous breakdown, she called me at work, excited about her accomplishment. She managed to deliver a package to our neighbor's house a few doors down! It was about 150 feet, and she had to stop twice to sit on the curb before making it there.

By now, several years after the nervous breakdown, she and I take brief walks of thirty minutes around the neighborhood nearly every day, with Agnes walking really slowly and stopping every minute or so for a break. She's still not back where she used to be and can't walk long distances; she does use a wheelchair when she has to do so, for example, in airports. Still, I firmly believe she will gradually improve to her previous level of capacity. All because we delayed our judgment and did not attribute her behavior to her personality but to the circumstances.

So how do you determine whether someone who cuts you off or yells at someone on the phone is a jerk? Glad you asked! Your best bet is to use the debiasing strategy of *making predictions about the future*. Predict whether the person who cut you off will cut off other people. If you observe such behavior, this evidence should increase your estimate of the likelihood of the person being a jerk, though you should leave open the possibility of him driving his pregnant wife to the hospital.

Solving the Fundamental Attribution Error Exercise

Please take a few minutes to journal your answers to these questions before going onward:

- How will you use *delaying our decisions and reactions* to fight the fundamental attribution error? Specifically, how will you implement this strategy? What challenges do you anticipate seeing in this implementation, and how will you overcome these challenges? What metrics will you use to measure your success in implementing this approach? What would the future of your relationships look like if you succeed in your implementation?

- How will you use *making predictions about the future* to fight the fundamental attribution error? Specifically, how will you implement this strategy? What challenges do you anticipate seeing in this implementation, and how will you overcome these challenges? What metrics will you use to measure your success in implementing this approach? What would the future of your relationships look like if you succeed in your implementation?

Group Attribution Error

Such snap judgments misattributing the reasons for behaviors also apply to our evaluations of broad groups, in what is known as the "group attribution error." This error comes in two forms: either when we perceive the characteristics of an individual member of a group to reflect the group as a whole or vice versa when we perceive the group's overall preferences to determine the preferences of individuals within that group.[38]

In the savanna, it was beneficial to our survival to make snap judgments about the tie-in between group and individual, regardless of the accuracy of such judgments. In fact, such judgments might have been more accurate in the prehistoric period of human evolution than in the modern world, as our ancestors all lived in small tribes. Members depended—very much—on the tribe for their survival, and members of a tribe shared many characteristics, above all loyalty to the tribe. So in the savanna environment, it was a safer bet that if you observed the behavior of a member of a certain tribe, their behavior largely reflected the overall perspective of their tribe; in turn, if you knew some details about the preferences of a specific tribe, you could have a relatively confident estimate of how a member of that tribe would behave.

That's not the case in the modern world. Our society is incredibly complex and diverse. The kind of group affiliations we have now—ethnicity, gender, sexuality, class, culture, religion, political ideology, profession, geographical location—produce multifaceted identities. It's a very poor bet that someone of the same ethnicity, gender, class, and so on will strongly resemble other people of the same group affiliation; likewise, it's equally irrational to use group affiliation to make confident judgments about a member of that group.

Tragically, those old instincts still dominate our judgments in the modern world. Group attribution error is one of the most important factors in stereotyping.

Let's say a small family-owned hardware shop hires a Pakistani employee for the first time ever. Now, imagine this Pakistani employee doesn't work out due to chronic lateness, and the owner eventually lets this employee go. What's the likelihood that the owner will hire another Pakistani employee? For most people—unless they deliberately watch out for this problem—it would be much lower than hiring the first Pakistani! The owner would now tend to attribute lateness to all Pakistanis as a group whether it's true or not.

Hey, I fall for the group attribution error too. I suffer from occasional back pain. Seeking a solution, I went to a chiropractor a few years ago. He cracked my back, and I left worse off than I came. I tried another chiropractor and had a similar experience. After that, I swore off chiropractors as useless and went to physical therapy and other treatments. However, my friend's dad is a chiropractor, and she convinced me to try him out, promising he doesn't do back cracking.

Well, the only thing he cracked was jokes. He was great, his methods much more effective than any other treatment I had had previously. He found the specific muscles that were out of whack in my back, relieved them, and prescribed very specific and targeted exercises, unlike the physical therapists who recommended a broad set of general exercises. I'm glad I didn't let the group attribution error undermine that valuable relationship for me.

Have you ever gone church shopping (or secular values–based group shopping for nonbelievers)? For those not familiar with the practice, it involves visiting various churches to see whether each church is a good fit. I've spoken to many folks who told me about one negative experience they had with a church member that led them to cross that church off their list. Knowing about the group attribution error, you can recognize the irrational nature of this kind of behavior: an individual member of a congregation is hardly representative of the whole. Those folks gave up potentially valuable relationships by making this error.

What about the reverse, a perception that the beliefs and attitudes of a whole group represent those beliefs of an individual member of the whole group? Stereotyping applies here as well.

For instance, as someone who comes from a culturally Jewish background, I'm all too aware that many people still believe the demonstrably false myth about Jewish greediness. They wrongly assume that any Jew they meet must be greedy.

In reality, the 2017 Giving USA report found that the average Jewish household donates $2,526 to charity yearly, compared to $1,749 for Protestants, which is the largest religious denomination in the US. This disparity is not simply a result of income difference: among households earning less than $50,000, about 60 percent of Jewish households donated some money to charity, by comparison to 46 percent for households that are not Jewish.

Moreover, Jews regularly give to non-Jewish causes. For example, the report showed that 54 percent of Jews were more likely to make a donation to social-service charities than to their religious congregation; the comparative number for those who are not Jewish is 41 percent. Still, the myth about Jewish greed is persistent and powerfully shapes perceptions of Jews.

The same problem plagues political discussions. Too often, when we hear the label "democrat" or "republican," we assume the other person shares all the views of the relevant political party. In reality—whatever your political affiliation—you probably disagree with at least one and likely many more planks of your political party's platform. Based on your own experience, you should assume that any other person with whom you speak similarly does not agree with at least some points from their own party.

Stepping back from this assumed agreement can greatly facilitate positive relationships with people who are not aligned with you politically. You might consider having a conversation about what aspects of their chosen party's platform they don't fully support. And you should definitely be skeptical of extremist caricatures drawn of political partisans, such as the idea that conservatives hate the poor and liberals want to destroy capitalism.

Group Attribution Error Exercise

Please take a few minutes to journal your answers to these questions before going onward:

- Where have you fallen into the group attribution error in your life? How has doing so harmed your relationships? Where have you seen other people fall for the group attribution error in their lives? How has doing so harmed their relationships?

Solving the Group Attribution Error

A useful debiasing technique to addressing the group attribution error involves *considering alternative explanations and options.* As an example, the errors made by the people who were church shopping (described above) easily give way when evaluating alternative explanations. Rather than immediately feeling rejected by one individual who didn't want to talk during coffee hour after a sermon, consider whether it's possible that this person was having a bad day and maybe wanted some peace and quiet or perhaps was unusually struck by the sermon and wanted to think about it. Try to approach other folks, especially ones who seem like they're standing in a group and talking to others. Ask them politely to join their conversation and, at a break in the conversation, tell them you're church shopping and ask them about the church. That way, you can learn both about how welcoming the people are and about the church as a whole.

The Pakistani employee's lateness presents another opportunity to use this tool. An intuitive gut reaction hypothesis might be to attribute lateness as a characteristic to all Pakistanis. An alternative explanation is that the employee's country of origin and cultural upbringing didn't cause the employee to be chronically late. How can you figure out which explanation is correct?

While it can be quite costly, in terms of money and resources, to hire another Pakistani and evaluate their time management skills, you may want to research the question of time management and Pakistanis online. Believe me, if this were a problem, there would be significant commentary on the Internet about it, as there is on the loose sense of time in Italy. My Google search of Pakistani and "chronic lateness" suggests it's not true.

Getting an external perspective on the situation offers another method to debias the fundamental attribution error. My friend's external perspective on my negative experience with chiropractors really helped address my back pain. And hey, to be fair to chiropractors, two negative experiences are a quite small sample size to make an evaluation on a whole profession. The whole experience caused me to scale back my intuitively quick judgments of professions.

An external perspective also helps in the case of the myth of Jewish greed. In this case, the Giving USA 2017 report offers an excellent and completely neutral external perspective. They simply crunch the numbers and, if you wish, you could look through the whole 422-page report to verify its accuracy. This external perspective offers resounding proof that Jews are somewhat more altruistic than the average American, including the average Protestant. As someone who's culturally Jewish, I know about and appreciate the strong emphasis in Judaism on charitable giving and was not surprised by this finding. (A disclaimer: While culturally Jewish, I do not follow Judaism and am a member of a Unitarian Universalist Church.)

Solving the Group Attribution Error Exercise

Please take a few minutes to journal your answers to these questions before going onward:

- How will you use *considering alternative explanations* to solve the group attribution error? Specifically, how will you implement this strategy? What challenges do you anticipate seeing in this implementation, and how will you overcome these challenges? What metrics will you use to measure your success in implementing this approach? What would the future of your relationships look like if you succeed in your implementation?

- How will you use *considering external perspectives* to fight the group attribution error? Specifically, how will you implement this strategy? What challenges do you anticipate seeing in this implementation, and how will you overcome these challenges? What metrics will you use to measure your success in implementing this approach? What would the future of your relationships look like if you succeed in your implementation?

Ultimate Attribution Error

A final relevant cognitive bias, the *ultimate attribution error,* combines elements of the fundamental attribution error and the group attribution error. The ultimate attribution error causes us to misattribute problematic group behaviors to the internal characteristics of groups that we don't like as opposed to external circumstances and vice versa for groups we like.[39]

Here's a clear example of ultimate attribution error. Organizations often bring me in as a speaker on diversity and inclusion since cognitive biases are an important reason for discriminatory behavior. When I share in speeches that black Americans suffer from police harassment and violence at a much higher rate than white people, some participants (usually white) occasionally try to defend the police by claiming that black people are more violent and likely to break the law than whites. They thus attribute police harassment to the internal characteristics of black people (implying that it is deserved), not to the external context of police behavior. In reality—as I point out in my response to these folks—research shows that black people are harassed and harmed by police at a much higher rate for the same kind of activity. A white person walking by a cop, for example, is statistically much less likely to be stopped and frisked than a black one; at the other end of things, a white person resisting arrest is much less likely to be violently beaten than a black one.[40] In other words, statistics show that the higher rate of harassment and violence against black Americans by police is due to the prejudice of the police officers, at least to a large extent.[41]

However, I am careful to clarify that this discrimination is not necessarily intentional. Sometimes, it indeed is deliberate, with white police officers consciously believing that black Americans deserve much more scrutiny than whites. At other times, the discriminatory behavior results from autopilot system processes that the police officer would not consciously endorse. Such unconscious negative associations are called "implicit bias," and most police officers suffer from implicit bias.[42] Note that implicit bias is not one of the cognitive biases; it is a distinct term belonging to the same category of social biases as racism, sexism, and so on, which should not be confused with cognitive biases.

Interestingly, research shows that many black police officers have an unconscious prejudice against other black people, perceiving them in a more negative light than white people when evaluating potential suspects. This implicit bias carried by many, not all, black police officers helps show that such prejudices come—at least to a significant extent—from internal cultures within police departments, rather than preexisting racist attitudes before someone joins a police department. Such cultures

are perpetuated by internal norms, policies, and training proce-
dures, and any police department wishing to address implicit bias
needs to address internal culture first and foremost rather than
attributing racism to individual officers. In other words, instead of
saying it's a few bad apples in a barrel of overall good ones, the key
is recognizing that implicit bias is a systemic issue and that the
structure and joints of the barrel need to be fixed.

The crucial thing to highlight is that there is no shame or
blame in implicit bias, as it's not stemming from any fault in the
individual. This no-shame approach decreases the fight, freeze, or
flight defensive response among reluctant audiences, helping
them hear and accept the issue.

With these additional statistics and discussion of implicit
bias, the issue is generally settled. Still, from their subsequent
behavior, it's clear that some of these audience members don't
immediately internalize this evidence. It's much more comforting
for their autopilot system to believe that police officers are right
and anyone targeted by police deserves it; in turn, they are highly
reluctant to accept the need to focus more efforts and energy on
protect black Americans from police violence due to the struc-
tural challenges facing these groups.[43]

The issue of implicit bias doesn't match their intuitions, and
thus they reject this concept, despite extensive and strong evidence for its pervasive role in policing. It takes a series of subsequent follow-up conversations and interventions to move the
needle.[44] A single training is almost never sufficient, both in my
experience and according to research.[45] The lack of willingness to
acknowledge prejudice by police is an example of the ultimate
attribution error going the other way, where people don't want to
acknowledge that groups they like might have some negative
characteristics.[46]

Ultimate Attribution Error Exercise

Please take a few minutes to journal your answers to these questions before going onward:

- Where have you fallen into the ultimate attribution error in your life? How has doing so harmed your relationships? Where have you seen other people fall for the group attribution error in their lives? How has doing so harmed their relationships?

Solving the Ultimate Attribution Error

To solve the ultimate attribution error, it really helps to *consider other people's points of view* as a debiasing tool. If you looked through the eyes of a police officer, would you learn they were deliberately prejudiced against black people or instead were one of many fine police officers combating such prejudices within the ranks? Either is possible, or something in between, for instance someone who suffers from implicit bias while trying to fight it within themselves. When learning about any charged policing situation—such as a white police officer stopping a young black male driver—we can't be confident about the perspective of the police officer since we can't read their mind. Accepting humbly our inability to be correct with a snap judgment by our autopilot system helps us get to a place where we can use a more intentional system approach relying on evidence.

Still, we shouldn't approach a racially charged policing action as though we have no preexisting knowledge and should instead rely on the debiasing tool of *probabilistic thinking*. Say you find out about a black person being assaulted by a police officer. Independent of any other knowledge, it's hard to form a conclusion about whether the person's behavior justified the police officer's response or not. However, you know now—having read the information in the previous section—that police violence toward black people tends to be much more severe than that toward white people for the same behaviors. Therefore, your prior probability should be that it's more likely that the police officer's response was excessive. Then, as the details of the incident unfold, you should update your beliefs to match the evidence, while keeping the overall base rate in mind.

Solving the Ultimate Attribution Error Exercise

Please take a few minutes to journal your answers to these questions before going onward:

- How will you use *considering other people's points of view* to address the ultimate attribution error? Specifically, how will you implement this strategy? What challenges do you anticipate seeing in this implementation, and how will you overcome these challenges? What metrics will you use to measure your success in implementing this approach? What would the future of your relationships look like if you succeed in your implementation?

- How will you use *probabilistic thinking* to fight the ultimate attribution error? Specifically, how will you implement this strategy? What challenges do you anticipate seeing in this implementation, and how will you overcome these challenges? What metrics will you use to measure your success in implementing this approach? What would the future of your relationships look like if you succeed in your implementation?

Conclusion

All the debiasing techniques described in this chapter can be used on each of the three related attribution-error cognitive biases. Different methods work best depending on the situation at hand. By trying out and learning all the techniques, you will gain an appreciation of which tool to deploy in any given situation. The same principle applies to all other debiasing strategies described in future chapters: they apply to all the biases described in each chapter.

The most critical thing to take away from this chapter is that we make dangerous judgment errors of misattributing observed behaviors to the inherent characteristics of individuals or groups as opposed to their current circumstances. Doing so can be devastating for our relationships. Making a negative assumption about your date just because you see them yelling once on the phone can prevent you from having a wonderful romance. Presuming all chiropractors are bad from a small sample size can prevent much-needed pain relief. Judging an employee's ethnicity as responsible for problematic behavior results in a smaller pool of potential hires, giving your competitors an edge. Failing to appreciate the dangers of implicit bias perpetuates systemic injustice and prejudice in our society. Don't let yourself and those around you suffer these consequences by addressing attribution errors using the effective debiasing techniques discussed in this chapter.

Attribution errors are only one of the ways our minds our messed up. In the next chapter, we'll discuss cognitive biases around having an unrealistically positive perception of ourselves in comparison to others, which as you can imagine harms relationships greatly.

While I know it's tempting to go on and read more about this topic, for those who haven't yet completed the exercises in this chapter, I really urge you to go back and journal your answers to the questions in this chapter. You're only getting a small fraction of the benefit from reading this book if you don't invest the time in doing these exercises. So do yourself and those you care about—the people with whom you want to preserve good relationships or cultivate better ones—the favor of doing the exercises now, not later! And remember to check out the book's website for additional resources on this and other topics: http://disasteravoidanceexperts.com/blindspots.

CHAPTER 3

Are We Really Better?

Do you remember the song "Anything You Can Do (I Can Do Better)" by Irving Berlin? Originally composed for the 1946 Broadway musical *Annie Get Your Gun*, this duet involves a male and female singer claiming they can do anything and everything better than the other person. If you didn't see the musical, you might recall this song from covers of it performed by Barbra Streisand, or perhaps a 1997 commercial starring Michael Jordan and Mia Hamm, or maybe when Miss Piggy sang it in *The Muppet Show*, or one of the other iterations of this tune.

Why did this infectious song get so popular? A part of its popularity owes to the fact that our autopilot system sings the same tune in the back of our heads. A part of your mind—as well as my mind and everyone else's mind—believes we are better than everyone else, in every important way.

Sure, when I say it outright like that, you might deny that you believe it. Indeed, your intentional system, the self-reflective part of you, might not consciously endorse this claim. Still, at some level, your autopilot believes the world revolves around you. It tells you that you are the best and most important person in the world. Here's a secret: the same thing happens to the autopilot systems of all the other billions of people on Earth. What's the probability that, out of the nearly 8 billion people, you are objectively better than everyone else? Not high, right?

Here's another secret: you can't consciously stop this belief. A part of your autopilot will go on believing this notion even if you try to tell yourself you're not. You're only speaking to your intentional system when you do so, not your autopilot system.

Besides being ineffective, telling yourself that truth too much can cause negative feelings, and there's no real need to stop a module of your autopilot system from having this belief. What you do need to do is ensure that your intentional system understands that this belief does not reflect objective reality.

Using your intentional system in that fashion can address the damaging consequences of this incorrect mental pattern for your relationships. After all, being too full of yourself can devastate your romantic relationships, your friendships, your work life, and your civic and political engagement.

Does it feel uncomfortable to hold in your head the contradiction between the intentional system's recognition that the world does not revolve around you and the autopilot system's quiet but insistent feeling that it does? I hear you. I remember learning about the multiple contradictions in my head when first studying the harmful consequences of cognitive biases in my PhD program. I felt especially disappointed to learn that many of these irrational patterns can't be eradicated, only controlled.

What helped me was inspiration from a seemingly unlikely source, a line from poet Walt Whitman's poem "Song of Myself." In the poem, Whitman wrote "Do I contradict myself? Very well then, I contradict myself, (I am large, I contain multitudes)."[47]

That line truly resonated with me. It opened my eyes to the realization that I don't need to be fully consistent internally. After all, as I learned in graduate school and described in the first chapter, our perception of a sense of self is simply a mental construct, a comforting and mythical story that our mind tells us to help us function. The reality is that each of us consists of many mental processes that sometimes compete with each other, and we can notice the myth of a coherent and consistent self when we observe the kind of contradiction described by Whitman.

Moreover, while the science behind this insight is new, deep thinkers like Whitman intuitively grasped this complexity long ago, I realized. Whitman's poem made me recognize that the challenges I struggled with—of holding contradictory ideas in my head at once—were faced by many people in the past. And if they can do it, I can do it too—anything you can do, I can do better, right?

Illusory Superiority

As you have by now guessed, the mental pattern I described is one of the typical thinking errors we all have. "Illusory superiority" is the name behavioral scientists use for the cognitive bias that leads us to overestimate our positive qualities and discount negative ones.[48] Illusory superiority represents a specific form of the broader cognitive bias known as the "overconfidence effect," in which we tend to be way too confident about our evaluations of reality.[49]

The benefit of illusory superiority from an evolutionary perspective is clear. If I believe myself superior to others—the most important person in the world—it's natural for me to do my best not only to survive but also to pass on my genes. Those who did not have such overconfidence about their competence and characteristics did not work as hard to succeed in the genetic Russian roulette. We are the descendants of those who survived and thrived, and illusory superiority is part of our evolutionary heritage.

That doesn't mean every single reader of this book will be plagued by illusory superiority in all life areas, but research shows that the vast majority of us are overconfident about our awesomeness in life areas of importance to us. For those worried about whether I'm talking about research only done on American psychology undergraduate students, relax. The research on this topic involved extensive cross-cultural comparisons. When I originally learned of this research, I assumed that Americans, British, and others from more individualistic cultures would show the greatest overconfidence compared to other cultures, especially collectivist cultures with a greater respect for group conformity and personal humility. I was surprised to learn that Chinese, Malaysian, and Indonesian participants—who belonged to more collectivist cultures— showed more overconfidence than British and American participants.[50] I'm not sure why, but that's the kind of counterintuitive result that it's important to accept and internalize into our worldviews rather than sticking with unwarranted cultural stereotypes.

How can illusory superiority play out in relationships? Consider Tom and Mike as an example. They had been dating for a couple of months before Tom's lease ran out on his apartment and the landlord raised the rates. Mike, who inherited his house from his parents, invited Tom to move in with him, and Tom gratefully accepted.

Living together often reveals our worst qualities. Many of us can keep them hidden during the relatively brief interactions of a date, but cohabiting is another story. The close quarters and extended periods of time spent with each other loosens inhibitions, which proved to be the case for Tom and Mike. Mike soon started displaying an arrogant attitude about his better-paying job, making snide remarks about Tom's admittedly worse financial situation. Mike pressured Tom to take on more house chores and started offering to pay for Tom's meals and other bills with what Tom described as "an arrogant attitude." Tom tried to point this out to Mike, but the latter refused to listen, dismissing Tom's concerns.

Eventually, Tom grew so uncomfortable with Mike's increasingly arrogant attitude— both regarding finances and Mike's unwillingness to listen—that Tom decided to end the relationship, finding a place with a roommate instead. Tom told me this story after attending one of my speeches when I mentioned the dangers of illusory superiority for relationships. This cognitive bias frequently breeds inflated self-perceptions in romantic relationships, where one partner in a relationship falsely believes and exhibits the attitude that "I am too good for them" or "they are not worthy of me." It's even worse when both partners suffer from illusory superiority or more than two partners in a polyamorous relationship. Then, you get into a competition of each partner trying to top the other in who is the best, almost always leading to the end of a relationship. If it's only one person engaging in this behavior, you at least have some hope of addressing the problem if the other partner is willing to listen—unlike Mike.

If you have a large family, as I do, you might recall family holiday dinners where someone dominates the conversation, offering confident opinions on a topic they falsely believe they know more about than everyone else at the table. I remember a particularly bad birthday dinner in a Miami restaurant with my Eastern European family members, where some of the older ones confidently pontificated on US politics. Unfortunately, their pronouncements stemmed from watching Russian-language TV stations controlled by the Russian government. While I choose to prioritize maintaining cordial relationships over arguing with Putin-brainwashed family members, others argued with their deluded relatives, leading to much drama and long-lasting hurt feelings.

Speaking of politics, the problem of illusory superiority does grave harm to our political engagement and thus our relationships on a society-wide level. We tend to perceive our political evaluations and decision making as better than reality and see the assessments and choices of those who don't belong to our camp as worse than they really are. As a result, we often get into heated debates with those on the other side by trying to convince them of our perspective, not realizing all along that our viewpoint is much weaker than it seems. We have the same attitude toward politicians we support and vice versa for those we don't support. When's the last time you saw some headlines critical of your favorite politician and chose to skip the article? It's only natural to do so, as such information makes us uncomfortable, going against our gut reactions. Yet it's this natural tendency—combined with the multitude of low-quality news sources nowadays that provide us with comforting but often inaccurate information—that plays a fundamental role in the polarization and post-truth politics we see in our country today.[51]

Illusory superiority often harms performance in the workplace as well. Don't you hate the know-it-all work colleague who loudly proclaims they know the right course of action after reading a couple of reports? It's even worse when the colleague is your supervisor. Unfortunately, most corporate environments reward bosses who make a dozen decisions a minute—including huge ones—without looking into the matter in any depth and solely relying on their intuitions and gut reactions. Research suggests that such decision making often leads to business catastrophes.[52] Yet this type of illusory superiority is sought out by boards of directors and subordinates who want to believe that the company's leader knows it all.[53]

At no time in my life did the siren song of illusionary superiority prove as tempting as after my wife Agnes had a nervous breakdown in July 2014. Prior to that, we were roughly even in our contributions to our relationship and household. We both contributed approximately equal amounts of emotional support for each other when the other had emotional turmoil as well as did things that contributed positive emotions to our relationship. Likewise, we supported household finances and did chores in a way that felt equal for our situation.

The situation changed drastically after the nervous breakdown. Agnes couldn't work anymore, putting me in the role of the sole breadwinner. She also was unable to do the vast majority of house chores, leaving me to manage them or let them slide (the dust bunnies grew fat and happy). Even more problematically, she could no longer offer me meaningful emotional support, and I had to provide much more emotional support for her. Her changed personality and wildly fluctuating moods brought much more negativity to the relationship compared to the positive emotions she brought previously.

Illusory Superiority Exercise

You're too good to do this exercise, right? You'll get the point anyway, so why not skip it and go onward? Congrats for demonstrating illusory superiority in action! Don't let this irony happen to you, and take out your journal to answer the questions below. Please don't go onward until you do, as research shows that addressing cognitive biases requires understanding and self-reflecting about how they impact you.

- Where have you fallen into illusory superiority in your life? How has doing so harmed your relationships? Where have you seen other people fall for illusory superiority in their lives? How has doing so harmed their relationships?

Solving Illusory Superiority

Burdened by all the extra weight of being the sole caretaker for Agnes and aghast at her drastically altered personality and lack of capacity for emotional support, it was only natural and intuitive for my autopilot system to feel superior in our relationship. Letting such illusory superiority take hold and believing that my gut reactions spoke the truth could have led to the end of our relationship.

Fortunately, I was well aware of the problem of illusory superiority and determined to fight this tendency. The debiasing strategy of *considering the other person's perspective* really helped. Agnes and I had long conversations about the situation. She opened up about her internal experience of the nervous breakdown and its consequences, her gratitude to me for my role in supporting her, and her deep regret for the strains on me and our relationship caused by her condition. Putting myself in her shoes gave me a deeper understanding and appreciation not only for her suffering, but also her internal strength and profound determination to recover and rebuild, which gave me much hope for the future. It was gratifying to see my hope turn to reality as she recovered, slowly but surely. I'm not sure how well I would have done had I been in her shoes, and I sure hope I never have to find out.

For another example, what if Mike stopped to think about how his comments made Tom feel? What if Mike actually listened to what Tom was trying to say about Mike's arrogant attitude about finances, instead of brushing it off? They might still be together, instead of Tom moving out, which Mike took pretty hard from what Tom told me. Mike's excessive focus on finances and his overconfidence that he held the upper hand in the relationship cost him dearly.

Considering alternative explanations and options represents another powerful debiasing strategy to address illusory superiority. What if you don't know it all on a work question? What if your gut reactions aren't steering you in the right direction in your professional career?

Think it can't happen to you? Terrible judgment calls happen to some of the most prominent business leaders in the world. Consider the time when Elon Musk tweeted on August 7, 2018, that he is "considering taking Tesla private at $420. Funding secured." The tweet prompted much consternation among investors and spurred an investigation by the SEC, which found that the claim of secured funding was false. Musk had to pay a $20 million fine and step down from his position as chair of Tesla's board of directors.

You might be tempted to dismiss this example because Tesla is such a new car company and Musk is well-known for putting his foot in his mouth. Let's use another example of an old and conservative car company: Volkswagen. This German car giant acknowledged in September 2015 that it used cheating software in its VW and Audi cars to give false readings when the cars underwent emission tests. Known as "Dieselgate," the revelation shook up the car industry and led to the resignation of CEO Martin Winterkorn, along with several other top leaders. According to investigators who charged Winterkorn with fraud and conspiracy in May 2018, the former Volkswagen CEO apparently approved the use of the "defeat device" to falsify emissions standards. VW's stock fell more than 40 percent over the next few days, and the overall cost of the scandal to the company has been estimated at over $20 billion.

These examples are just two very public ones of a multitude of horrendous decisions made by top business leaders in the grip of illusory superiority. What hope do we have if we let illusory superiority retain its grip, instead of considering the alternative that we may not be as supercilious as we think we are in the workplace? We should especially watch out when we are tempted to show off our smarts, such as when we use words like "supercilious"

supercilious - behaving or looking as though one thinks they are superior to others when more commonplace and widely understood terms like "superior" are available.

The same mindset fix applies to political engagement. Consider the alternative scenario that your intuitive political judgment is just as flawed as that of all the other billions of people in the world. Hold in your mind, which like Walt Whitman's is large and contains multitudes, the idea that your favorite politicians may be less stellar than they intuitively seem to our tribal brain. This dose of humility can do much to address the polarization and post-truth politics that are now destroying the health of democracy, in the US and around the globe.

Solving Illusory Superiority Exercise

Please take a few minutes to journal your answers to these questions before going onward:

- How will you use *considering other people's points of view* to fight illusionary superiority? Specifically, how will you implement this strategy? What challenges do you anticipate seeing in this implementation, and how will you overcome these challenges? What metrics will you use to measure your success in implementing this approach? What would the future of your relationships look like if you succeed in your implementation?

- How will you use *considering alternative explanations and options* to fight illusionary superiority? Specifically, how will you implement this strategy? What challenges do you anticipate seeing in this implementation, and how will you overcome these challenges? What metrics will you use to measure your success in implementing this approach? What would the future of your relationships look like if you succeed in your implementation?

Social Comparison Bias

You might have heard the phrase "keeping up with the Joneses," referring to trying to avoid falling behind your neighbors or other community members economically or culturally. You can see it in action when one of your neighbors gets a nice new car, and the next week, two of your neighbors get even better new cars. Perhaps you attend your church, and someone brags about their son's recent successful piano recital; next time, you hear that five other parents enrolled their kids in piano class.

Being tribal animals, we compare ourselves to those we perceive as part of our tribe. We compete with each other in activities and possessions that bring social status, both one-upping gains made by others and, sadly, often tearing down others who have it better than us. This intuitive tendency that harms so many relationships bears the name "social comparison bias."[54]

In the tribal setting of the savanna, it's understandable how the social comparison bias helped our ancestors survive and flourish. The higher their status in the tribe, the more likely they were to secure access to resources that enabled them to not simply to survive, but also to pass on their genes since better social status and resources made them a more appealing mating partner. In other words, we are the descendants of those who excelled at social status competition, a trait that frequently hurts us and our relationships in our modern environment.

Think about the original neighbor who got a great new car. The other neighbors feel jealousy and resentment toward that neighbor, regardless of whether they consciously realize their underlying autopilot system's experience. These feelings hurt the quality of their neighborly relationships. Then, they go out and spend money on an even better car, a purchase that harms their pocketbooks since they likely did not plan to buy the vehicle. So be wary of either getting a new flashy consumer good if you want to prevent jealousy and resentment or of purchasing one because you saw someone who got one, as in both cases, you might be falling into the social comparison bias.

The same problem applies to the piano recital. Bragging about your son's accomplishment induces similar feelings of jealousy and resentment, hurting relationships. In turn, if you're one of the parents pushing your son to take piano lessons, watch out: your son might feel resentment and frustration, which may harm your relationship with him.

In friendships, the social comparison bias may lead us to tear down and undermine those who we perceive as having better qualities than we do. In high school (before I got into the research on avoiding dangerous judgment errors), I was part of a clique of male friends who exhibited this behavior (myself included, I shamefully admit). We would rag on each other, especially when one of us got ahead of the others, whether academically, financially, or in romantic relationships. Such behavior inhibited all of us, as I now realize, from being our best selves. Over time, as I wised up to the harm that such friendship tendencies brought to my life, I left those relationships behind, instead developing friendships with men and women who provide me with a healthy support network. While such tendencies are common among men, they are apparently even more widespread among women, as I learned from the research on this topic and the stories of my female friends.[55]

While the social comparison bias doesn't harm all workplaces, I've seen many environments where it does. In a mid-size software firm that provided a variety of business services, the performance evaluation structure and internal culture strongly incentivized intense competition among teams of software engineers. While some competition may be healthy, the situation at this company was growing increasingly toxic, harming product quality and customer service. A case in point, innovations crucial for improving the firm's product quality were kept within teams instead of being shared widely within the company. Another problem: if a team of engineers did not have needed expertise and tried to reach out to other teams, they were often rebuffed. Likewise, software engineers refused to engage in customer service, perceiving it as a low-prestige activity and focusing instead on competing with fellow engineers on high-prestige technical innovations.

Brought in as a consultant to address this issue, I worked with the leadership to change the performance evaluation structure to incentivize collaboration. For instance, prior to the intervention, the bonus pool was shared among teams solely based on team performance compared to other teams, which incentivized an "every team for itself" mentality. Afterward, 30 percent of the bonus reflected how much each team helped other teams, with teams rating other teams on a company-wide survey before the distribution of the bonus. Similarly, promotions and raises were changed to reflect how much each individual engineer helped others within the organization, especially in customer service. To address internal culture, company messaging focused on praising internal collaboration, particularly customer service, and executives modeled such behaviors, with each top-level leader taking some time to interact with customers. Over twelve months, these reforms led to a much healthier internal culture, conducive to mutual collaboration and customer service, greatly improving relationships in that company.

Social Comparison Bias Exercise

Please take a few minutes to journal your answers to these questions before going onward:

- Where have you fallen into the social comparison bias in your life? How has doing so harmed your relationships? Where have you seen other people fall for the social comparison bias in their lives? How has doing so harmed their relationships?

Solving the Social Comparison Bias

You can rely on the debiasing strategy of *probabilistic thinking* as a means of addressing the social comparison bias. When tempted to keep up with the Joneses—whether in culture, consumer goods, or otherwise—consider the probabilities for the impact on your relationships and other life areas. Does your autopilot system feel that matching your neighbors, coworkers, or fellow church (synagogue, mosque, secular group) members with the purchase of a new car (or patio furniture, gas grill, flat-screen TV, or other form of conspicuous consumption) would make you happier and improve your relationships? How about engaging yourself or your children in a cultural activity after seeing others around you do so?

What's the probability that you're right? Put a number on that probability. Do you think it's 90 percent, 70 percent, 30 percent? Write it down in your journal.

Then, if you do choose to engage in that activity or make the purchase, look back after three months. Decide whether you made a good probabilistic estimate or not. You won't be surprised that most of the time we exaggerate the extent to which buying new consumer goods or engaging in cultural activities following our neighbors results in greater happiness and better relationships. In fact, research on the topic shows that increased consumption of material goods and most other forms of consumption don't make people happier; the only form of consumerism that increases happiness is leisure consumption, mainly because it improves what the scholars call "social connectedness," the unnecessarily supercilious term for relationships.[56] So it's relationships that make us happier, not consumerism or keeping up with the Joneses, according to the research.

Feel free to doubt my words, as well as the research. But before you get on the hedonistic treadmill, do make the probabilistic estimate I suggest above. After all, if you're right, what do you have to lose (except perhaps some delusions)?

Solving the Social Comparison Bias Exercise

Please take a few minutes to journal your answers to these questions before going onward:

• How will you use *probabilistic thinking* to fight the social comparison bias? Specifically, how will you implement this strategy? What challenges do you anticipate seeing in this implementation, and how will you overcome these challenges? What metrics will you use to measure your success in implementing this approach? What would the future of your relationships look like if you succeed in your implementation?

Egocentric Bias

In a phrase popularized by John F. Kennedy, "Victory has one hundred fathers and defeat is an orphan." This phrase encapsulates the "egocentric bias," people's tendency to ascribe to themselves more credit than is actually due for success while blaming others for failures.[57] If you play a team sport, you'll be well-familiar with this flawed mental pattern. I play doubles tennis regularly and always have to remember to avoid the intuitive desire to blame my partner when we lose a point. Similarly, you might notice the sometimes-extensive bickering among pro basketball players about who contributes most to the team. This bias is obviously not good for relationships with fellow team members.

Just as in sport teams, workplace teams systematically suffer from egocentric bias. It's often even worse than in sports. At least in the large majority of sports, you can observe directly what your teammates are doing; by contrast, in the workplace, many activities of fellow team members are invisible to others, and what's out of sight is out of mind. One of the first fixes I undertake in consulting projects involving team collaboration problems involves having each team member list the activities that led to some notable successes for the team (I always find it best to start with the one hundred fathers of successes rather than the orphan of failure since there's more positive emotions and team spirit around success). Teammates frequently express surprise over the extensive work done by other members of the team and grow to appreciate their contributions more. Another easy fix involves asking team members to distribute one hundred points anonymously to team members other than themselves in accounting for a project's success. As the facilitator, I add up and announce the results of this distribution, which never fails to surprise a number of team members, especially those suffering from strong illusory superiority along with egocentric bias.

Egocentric Bias Exercise

Please take a few minutes to journal your answers to these questions before going onward:

- Where have you fallen into the egocentric bias in your life? How has doing so harmed your relationships? Where have you seen other people fall for the egocentric bias in their lives? How has doing so harmed their relationships?

Solving the Egocentric Bias

Solving the egocentric bias requires us to take a step back and look at the situation from the outside in, using the debiasing strategy of *getting an external perspective*. Consider how you would evaluate your contribution to a work project or sport team's success differently if you stepped outside of yourself. Think about how much you contributed to it, and then reflect on what others did to make the success happen.

Then, take the harder step of dealing with the orphan of failure. Despite the discomfort in the pit of your stomach, grind down and list the things you did that contributed to the team project failure. It's not fun, but it's critical for dealing with egocentric bias and illusory superiority.

The debiasing tool of *setting a policy to guide our future self* in the future—whether as individuals, teams, or organizations—is sorely needed to solve the egocentric bias. For instance, consider the strategies described above that I used to help address the conflicts and tensions about which team members made the biggest contributions to project successes (and failures). It's an easy policy for you as an individual to reflect on the contributions of all of your team members. Similarly, it's easy for a team leader to have all team members list their contributions or an organization to make this approach a requisite component of team self-assessments. The same team or organization can have members distribute points to all team members except themselves to account for project success (and failure).

Solving the Egocentric Bias Exercise

Please take a few minutes to journal your answers to these questions before going onward:

- How will you use *getting an external perspective* to fight the egocentric bias? Specifically, how will you implement this strategy? What challenges do you anticipate seeing in this implementation, and how will you overcome these challenges? What metrics will you use to measure your success in implementing this approach? What would the future of your relationships look like if you succeed in your implementation?

- How will you use *setting policies to guide your future self* to fight the egocentric bias? Specifically, how will you implement this strategy? What challenges do you anticipate seeing in this implementation, and how will you overcome these challenges? What metrics will you use to measure your success in implementing this approach? What would the future of your relationships look like if you succeed in your implementation?

Conclusion

CEOs of large companies are at the top of the financial food chain in our society. They receive compensation packages that boggle the mind, in the dozens of millions of dollars. Moreover, they direct the financial might of companies worth in the dozens of billions. They had to make a series of terrific decisions to get to their positions.

Yet, even they make atrocious judgment errors due to illusory superiority. Tesla, for example, was worth over $50 billion when Musk made the tweet that cost him $20 million and his position as chair of Tesla's board of directors. Volkswagen was worth over $60 billion in 2015 when Winterkorn admitted and apologized for Dieselgate. Both of these mistakes stemmed from excessive confidence, and both cost the two men, and their companies, dearly.

When I coach CEOs and other business leaders, I highlight to them the dangers of falling into illusory superiority. The more success you have, the more danger you face from this problem. Yet research shows that all of us tend to be overconfident to some extent or other. We all need to be wary of illusory superiority, as well as social comparison bias and egocentric bias, if we want to protect ourselves, our relationships, and our organizations from disasters. For more techniques on protecting yourself, visit the book's website: http://disasteravoidanceexperts.com/blindspots.

Fortunately, if you do the exercises and consistently follow your plans to integrate the debiasing strategies that address these cognitive biases, you should be in good shape. To be clear, by "good shape," I am referring to your mental fitness. To protect yourself from cognitive biases, you need to exercise your mental muscles by practicing debiasing strategies daily in the same way you exercise physically to keep your body in good physical shape. After all, isn't your mind just as important as the rest of your body, and perhaps even more so?

In the next chapter, we'll shift from these individually oriented superiority biases to examining dangerous judgment errors around groups to which we belong. Stay tuned!

CHAPTER 4

The Danger of Tribalism

The football rivalry between the Ohio State University's Buckeyes in my hometown of Columbus, Ohio, and the University of Michigan's Wolverines is famous (or infamous if you're stuck in traffic when fans are going home after the big game). I had a chance to see this rivalry from the inside, having spent seven years as a professor at Ohio State, where I was contractually obligated to root for the Buckeyes (semi-kidding, semi-not).

The mood of my students—and the campus as a whole—strongly correlated with whether the Buckeyes won the big head-to-head game with the Wolverines. The positive emotions of pride and joy around our team were a wonder to behold. Less wonderful was the hate and disdain expressed toward the Wolverines, and the University of Michigan as a whole.

Yet these feelings didn't stay within the university environment. I was giving a talk in May 2018 on how dangerous judgment errors undercut diversity and inclusion at the annual conference on diversity and inclusion organized by the Columbus Area Human Resource Association. During my talk, with about one hundred HR professionals in the audience, I brought up the Buckeyes-Wolverines rivalry and asked these HR professionals to raise their hand if they would hire a Michigan fan.

Guess how many raised their hand. Write down your answer before going forward.

Before revealing the answer, let me highlight that these are top-notch professionals specifically trained to fight biases in hiring practices within themselves and within their organization as a whole. Moreover, they were attending a conference on diversity and inclusion so were steeped in the topic all day. They knew to be on guard against irrational discriminatory impulses.

Ready? The magic number of those who would hire a Michigan fan, out of about a hundred HR professionals in the audience, was three. Yes, you read that right, three.

So what's my point: You shouldn't wear your Michigan hat to a job interview in Columbus? Sure, but there's much actually much more to it than that.

Our tribal affiliations—the groups to which we feel a substantial sense of belonging—distort our judgments in ways that cause us to make dangerous errors that really damage our relationships. Thus, when I speak in Columbus and ask whether anyone in the audience would be willing to have a romantic partner, a neighbor, or a friend who is a Michigan fan, no more than 5 percent of the audience raises their hand, and frequently no one does. The same tribalism leads to discrimination around ethnicity, sex, gender, religion, age, politics, disability, geographic origins, and many other forms of group belonging. This chapter lays out the specific cognitive biases that harm to our relationships to help you spot and address such errors. We'll also go over the techniques you can use to fight the damage caused by these biases.

The Horns Effect

If we don't like some aspect of a person, particularly one that puts the individual in a group at odds with one to which we feel connected, we will evaluate that individual too harshly, a mental failure mode called the "horns effect."[58]

The horns effect explains the irrationally negative reactions of Columbus-area HR professionals toward Michigan fans as well as other forms of discrimination in the workplace. As an example, the large majority of US citizens treat those with foreign accents as less trustworthy than those who don't have a foreign accent.[59] After all, a foreign accent indicates "you're not from around here": in other words, you're not part of my tribe. In the savanna environment, those who didn't belong to our tribe meant danger. It helped our survival for our autopilot system to have an immediate suspicion of such people, leading us to downgrade them internally, usually without our conscious mind noticing anything occurring. The unfortunate fact that black Americans earn less than white Americans is explained not only by the institutional history of racism, but also by the horns effect of the overwhelmingly white bosses experiencing negative feelings toward blacks due to tribalism.[60]

The horns effect is more complex than tribalism, however: it also interacts with our perceptions of social hierarchies to cause us to rate those at the top of these hierarchies as better than those on the bottom. For instance, overweight applicants are rated negatively in job interviews.[61] There's no rational explanation for it: overweight people can do the job just as well as those who aren't. The explanation stems from the stigma against overweight people in our society, which places them lower than people who aren't overweight on the social hierarchy. You won't be surprised that women earn less than men, a result of still-existing harmful perceptions among many in the US that male breadwinners deserve a higher place on the social hierarchy than female ones.[62]

All of these forms of discrimination—whether based on race, gender/sexuality, physical attraction, weight, height—damage both workplace performance and relationships. Fortunately, there are legal ways to pursue discrimination based on the first two, but it's much harder to pursue legal action on the latter three and on many other forms of harmful discrimination, such as sports fandom.

Let's take an example of discrimination outside the workplace: sundown towns. Apparently, a number of US towns prohibited ethnic and racial minorities in the towns after sunset. This vile practice happened not only in the South, but throughout the country, and continued far longer than you might imagine. As an example, Darien, Connecticut, and Lake Forest, Illinois, both prohibited blacks and Jews from living in the city until 1990.[63] Such widespread discrimination in large areas still continues. You might be surprised to learn that on June 7, 2017, the National Association for the Advancement of Colored People warned blacks against traveling to Missouri, suggesting that if they must travel, they should keep bail money with them in case they are unfairly arrested. While overt sundown towns and areas have been fortunately done away with, some communities still discriminate covertly against minorities, doing much harm to relationships across racial and ethnic lines.

The horns effect can even cause splits within tribes when one tribal affiliation goes against another. A friend of mine who serves as a United Methodist pastor told me about how his denomination, with just under 7 million members in the US, is facing a great deal of internal turmoil over whether to permit same-sex weddings. This turmoil is taking place both between congregations and within congregations. Some churches express strong support for these weddings, some strong opposition, and others are divided on the matter. For example, my pastor friend—who supports such weddings—struggles to manage his congregation. Located in a conservative area, most of the members of his church oppose same-sex weddings. He works subtly to steer them toward greater tolerance through highlighting relevant passages in the

Bible and calling for the church to at least welcome LGBTQ members if not host their weddings. Yet his road is not easy, since so many members of his church feel a horns effect toward this issue. He doesn't want to drive away congregants by pushing too hard, while also giving his congregation an appropriate push in making sure that—to quote Martin Luther King, which my friend did—"The arc of the moral universe is long, but it bends toward justice." He told me about how many more tolerant people leave close-minded congregations to join more open churches, while some from more open-minded congregations witness close-minded members leave the congregation and even the denomination.

The challenge here is that the tribal belonging of United Methodism is at odds for many people with their political tribe. Many conservatives reject LGBTQ rights and try to oppose these rights however they can. These conservatives work within their church to deprive LGBTQ members of the right to a wedding. When they perceive themselves to be losing, some choose to renounce their congregation, even their denomination, as their tribal affiliation as conservatives is stronger than that of United Methodism.

At this point, I want to remind you once again that these social biases are not the same thing as cognitive biases. Cognitive biases are inherent features of the faulty wiring of our brains and explain why we make dangerously incorrect evaluations of reality that damage our relationships and other life areas. Social biases result from the consequences of these false perceptions, yet the specific social biases that arise in each society are determined by historical circumstances. For example, it's only the historical circumstances of sports rivalry that created such hatred between Wolverine and Buckeye fans. In turn, if you go back a few centuries you'll find that people now considered overweight were seen as more attractive, say in the art of Peter Paul Rubens

(1577–1640), and thin men and women would be low on the social hierarchy. Consider another example: if you move across space instead of time, you'll find that in India irrational discrimination focuses on the caste system, with Brahmins on the top and Dalits on the bottom.

So in every society, the horns effect will create some kind of irrational discriminatory social biases, yet the specific social biases will be particular to that society. We can only get out of this very harmful situation if we take specific and deliberate steps to combat the negative consequences of the horns effect, using strategies described in the next section.

I want to conclude by sharing that I'm not invulnerable to these dangerous judgment errors. It's funny to recall now that my biggest horns effect around my relationship with Agnes was her low interest in intellectual discussions. She's wicked smart, but when I met her in my last year of high school, I was disappointed that she was interested in pragmatic and practical issues, not abstract intellectual discussions. At the time, I derived a great deal of personal satisfaction and social status in my clique of fellow intellectually oriented high school friends from my discussion and debating skills; these abilities represented an integral part of my personal identity and group belonging. I was disappointed to learn that, while quite capable of holding her own in such discussions, when push comes to shove, she was not very interested in engaging in philosophizing. Given my own sense of tribal affiliations, her disinterest made it hard for me to feel that she was fully part of my tribe.

Horns Effect Exercise

I get it, you don't like doing the exercises. Some horns effects going on toward them, right? Well, this is one area where you don't want to let your gut lead you astray and make a bad decision for your relationships and other life areas. So take out your journal to answer the questions below. Please don't go onward until you do, as research shows that addressing cognitive biases requires understanding and self-reflecting about how they impact you.

- Where have you fallen into the horns effect in your life? How has doing so harmed your relationships? Where have you seen other people fall for the horns effect in their lives? How has doing so harmed their relationships?

Solving the Horns Effect

Delaying your reactions and judgment of others is a great debiasing strategy for dealing with horns effect. Take a mindful pause before passing judgment of new people you meet, especially if you feel a strong negative gut reaction around them. Think whether there's potential for unwarranted bias.

For example, in a work setting, if you're meeting a new business colleague, interviewing a potential employee, or attending a meeting with vendors, beware of the impact of physical attraction, height, body shape, accent, race, gender, and other notable physical factors. Remember that we tend to undervalue overweight people and those with foreign accents. Our gut doesn't give women and members of ethnic and racial minorities the credit they duly deserve. By noticing and delaying judgments, you can overcome your initial negative intuitions.

To further empower your efforts to resist the horns effect, try the debiasing tool of *making predictions about the future*. In work situations, when you have negative gut feelings about someone— especially in cases of first impressions about new people that you meet—make a prediction about that person. Is the overweight individual really going to perform poorly? Will that person with the French accent really turn out to be arrogant, or might that just be a culturally ingrained stereotype depicting the French as arrogant?

You won't know if you don't write it down and check the prediction later as we tend to forget bad guesses that we made in the past. Moreover, by predicting and making a commitment to check your prediction later, you can help yourself both be better calibrated and also have a clear opportunity to change your perspectives. Thus, you might shift how you think about people who are overweight or have foreign accents in general, as well as about the specific person you are working with in particular.

I'm very relieved that I didn't let the horns effect around Agnes's low interest in abstract conversations prevent the development of our relationship. Although distressed at her lack of engagement in intellectual discussions, I greatly appreciated her many other wonderful character traits. So I tried the strategy of making predictions about the future by making myself predict whether her disinterest would indeed prove problematic for me in six months from when I first seriously considered the question. I looked outside of our relationship for intellectual discussions. It proved surprisingly easy to satisfy that desire: with other friends, in clubs, in classes, in online forums, and many other venues. Yet the many other qualities she possessed, from emotional support and acceptance to appreciating my decidedly quirky humor to being an excellent collaborator on life projects, weren't something I could easily source outside of the relationship. In other words, the quality lacked by Agnes proved much less important in the relationship than I thought, and making a solid prediction worked wonderfully to address a horns effect area that I originally thought would be a huge problem.

Considering past experience, when assessed objectively and accurately, is another debiasing method that helps address the horns effect. If you're in a church, club, or other group debating a socially polarizing issue, reflect on what past experience suggests about the topic at hand. In the context of gay marriage and the Methodist Church, it's important to recognize that over time, our society has grown more supportive of gay rights and other civil rights. With this in mind, standing against civil rights will be very unlikely to benefit the Methodist Church in the long term. As such, it may be wise to get ahead of the curve and position itself for the future. You can apply the same mindset to debates on other issues.

Solving the Horns Effect Exercise

Please take a few minutes to journal your answers to these questions before going onward:

- How will you use *delaying your reactions and judgment* to fight the horns effect? Specifically, how will you implement this strategy? What challenges do you anticipate seeing in this implementation, and how will you overcome these challenges? What metrics will you use to measure your success in implementing this approach? What would the future of your relationships look like if you succeed in your implementation?

- How will you use *making predictions about the future* to fight the horns effect? Specifically, how will you implement this strategy? What challenges do you anticipate seeing in this implementation, and how will you overcome these challenges? What metrics will you use to measure your success in implementing this approach? What would the future of your relationships look like if you succeed in your implementation?

- How will you use *considering past experience* to fight the horns effect? Specifically, how will you implement this strategy? What challenges do you anticipate seeing in this implementation, and how will you overcome these challenges? What metrics will you use to measure your success in implementing this approach? What would the future of your relationships look like if you succeed in your implementation?

The Halo Effect

In contrast to the horns effect, when we feel a strong liking for one characteristic of someone, especially a trait that makes us feel like they're a part of a group to which we have a clear tribal affiliations, we will tend to have an excessively positive opinion of that person's other characteristics. This cognitive bias goes by the name "halo effect."[64]

The halo effect plays out in many areas of relationships, such as physical attraction. Our autopilot system drives us to feel this attraction toward those who match the aesthetic standards of beauty of the group that we see as our tribe.[65] In the savanna environment, those standards indicated potential mates who were at the top of the social hierarchy of the tribe: in other words, those best fit for our genes to be passed onward.

Unfortunately, the more we find someone physically attractive, the more we will overestimate all their other positive qualities and underestimate their negative ones. This unfortunate dynamic, one of many ways that the halo effect manifests itself, likely stems from a combination of the autopilot system's drive to have us mate with this person as well as the baseline predisposition we have to feel a positive association for those we feel are part of our tribe. As an example, research shows that we believe people whom we evaluate as more aesthetically pleasant to have a greater level of intelligence and social skills, regardless of the facts.[66] Here's another important finding: if we rate our romantic partner as more aesthetically attractive than ourselves, research shows we will be more likely to be submissive in the relationship.[67]

So keep that in mind if you are entering a relationship with someone whom you perceive as significantly more attractive than yourself. You're likely to overestimate their other qualities and will probably put up with more problematic behavior on their part.

The halo effect, just like the horns effect, has very negative impacts in the workplace. For example, those judged as more physically attractive are ranked better when employers evaluate potential employees.[68] It happens around the globe.[69] Those we see as more physically attractive earn more money.[70] Taller people are seen as better leaders, more worthy of respect, and as better performers, and you won't be surprised that taller people earn more money.[71] We are even more likely to give more attractive politicians jobs: voters are more likely to vote for politicians they find more politically attractive.[72] Of course, neither height nor physical attraction improve job performance, in business or politics, yet the subtle consequences of the halo effect cause these disparities.

Let's talk about another aspect of halo effect impacting relationships, specifically friendships. The halo effect sometimes masks friendships that no longer serve you well. I had two friends from high school who shared much of my tribal background, ranging from Eastern European culture to shared high school experiences. As I grew older, we experienced more and more tensions with each other as we pursued different life paths, and our values and personalities drifted apart.

Studying behavioral science and self-reflecting on my needs and wants in graduate school, I increasingly realized those friendships no longer served me well. Due to the halo effect, I was overestimating the positive qualities of those friends because of our shared group affiliations. These two friendships were eating up more of my energy and time than they were contributing to my life, which was especially problematic for me as an introvert who gets drained easily in social interactions and needs to spend extensive time alone to recover. This drain prevented me from having sufficient energy to seek out friendships that would be a better fit for my needs in my new life stage. Thus, I took deliberate steps to try to distance myself from them. It wasn't easy, especially since they didn't recognize the changing relationship dynamics and wanted to remain close for old times' sake. Still, "breaking up" with those friends was by far the best thing for both me and them in the long run.

What about you: Do you have any friends with whom more distance or a complete ending of the relationship might serve you well? Be honest with yourself, as the halo effect might make this a difficult question to answer.

Halo Effect Exercise

Please take out your journal to answer the questions below:

- Where have you fallen into the halo effect in your life? How has doing so harmed your relationships? Where have you seen other people fall for the halo effect in their lives? How has doing so harmed their relationships?

Solving the Halo Effect

Reflecting on the future and repeating scenarios offers an effective means of debiasing around the halo effect. Considering alternatives empowered me when I was reflecting on the two friends I had from high school. I recognized that the long-term friendships and sense of mutual tribal belonging might be exerting an unhelpful cloud of positivity on my relationships with them, even if the relationships might not be serving me well.

So I tried to consider alternative scenarios instead. Would I want to establish a friendship with either of the two now if I met them today, I asked myself? No, of course I wouldn't, I immediately answered: they're very different people, and we would not click at all. That immediate response provided strong evidence that the relationships did not serve me well.

I also considered alternative paths to the future. Would I want to have those relationships to help connect me to the past, or did they serve as anchors weighing me down to a history from which I wanted to free myself? In my situation at the time I was making the decision about the friendships, it was definitely the latter.

The same technique of considering alternatives helps address halos around physical attraction. Since you know that we tend to vote for politicians we perceive as more attractive—and if you want to prevent your choice from being weighed by that bias—try to imagine that your preferred candidate looks like the least attractive politician you know. Would you still vote for that person?

Want to see what your friends truly think about politics? Try this consider-the-alternative party trick. Find some statements that any politician can utter, and see whether your friends can identify who said them. For example, both the Republican US President Donald Trump and the Democratic US Senator Sherrod Brown from Ohio strongly criticized General Motors in 2018 for closing a factory in Ohio. See if your friends can differentiate the two. You'll find some interesting results (and might not be the most popular person at the party).

To get a more accurate assessment of the qualities of your romantic partner, you can consider where that person falls on your personal scale of aesthetic preferences. If the person is unusually attractive, recognize that you probably have an unrealistically high evaluation of their other qualities. Use the debiasing technique of *getting an external perspective* to help you calibrate yourself. Ask a friend who is not attracted to your romantic partner to evaluate that person on qualities that matter to you, such as empathy, judgment, intelligence, humor, dependability, and so on, on a scale of 1 to 10. Make your own assessments as well, independently from the friend who is helping you. If your assessments turn out to be substantially higher than those of your friend, watch out: you're falling for the halo effect.

Show me the numbers! Use the debiasing strategy of *setting a policy for your future self*, as well as for your team and your organization if you're in a leadership role, to evaluate colleagues, employees, vendors, and other business associates numerically using transparent and job-relevant criteria. Then, to address the intuitive halo effects associated with issues like height, weight, aesthetics, and people who belong or don't belong to your tribal group, adjust the numbers. If you're likely to experience halo effects—for instance, due to height, physical attraction, similar cultural background, attending the same college, having the same name, or other halo effect inducers—decrease your numerical evaluations of the other person (I suggest 30 percent as a rule of thumb). If you're likely to experience horns effects, increase your numerical evaluations of the other person by the same amount. As you get more practice at this numerical evaluation approach, change these adjustments to reflect your growing skill set and capacity in recognizing these biases.

Solving the Halo Effect Exercise

Please take a few minutes to journal your answers to these questions before going onward:

- How will you use *reflecting on the future and repeating scenarios* to fight the halo effect? Specifically, how will you implement this strategy? What challenges do you anticipate seeing in this implementation, and how will you overcome these challenges? What metrics will you use to measure your success in implementing this approach? What would the future of your relationships look like if you succeed in your implementation?

- How will you use *getting an external perspective* to fight the halo effect? Specifically, how will you implement this strategy? What challenges do you anticipate seeing in this implementation, and how will you overcome these challenges? What metrics will you use to measure your success in implementing this approach? What would the future of your relationships look like if you succeed in your implementation?

- How will you use *setting a policy for your future self* to fight the halo effect? Specifically, how will you implement this strategy? What challenges do you anticipate seeing in this implementation, and how will you overcome these challenges? What metrics will you use to measure your success in implementing this approach? What would the future of your relationships look like if you succeed in your implementation?

Conclusion

I hope you, like me, agree that the sundown town experience seems abhorrent now. Yet consider the nature of that past experience from today's perspective. Large communities adopted this approach, and did so proudly, with the support of many people still living today as I write these words in 2018. For a more recent and controversial change, take the example of accepting LGBTQ lifestyles as fully legitimate: indeed, the issue of gay marriage that divides the Methodist Church was confirmed as the law of the land in the US only in 2015. What are other issues that we see as a normal and everyday practice for which people living a decade or two from now might criticize us? Perhaps societal ethics will shift to seeing meat-eating as unacceptable? Perhaps driving gas-guzzling cars that pollute the environment will be out of bounds? Reflecting on the future of our society's ethics from the perspective of past experience is an excellent exercise for addressing horns effects and halo effects now. For more ideas on addressing horns and halo effects, see the book's website: http://disaster avoidanceexperts.com/blindspots.

Even if our gut reactions don't cause us to have unfounded negative reactions—and especially if they do—our relationships can still be brought down by communication difficulties. In the next chapter, we'll look at such challenges, the cognitive biases that cause them and how you can defend yourself from such dangerous judgment errors.

CHAPTER 5

Feeling, Thinking, and Talking Past Each Other

It was such a great date, thought George. Mary was so understanding and interested, what a wonderful listener! George told Mary all about himself. Mary truly got him, unlike so many other women he dated, he felt. She really cared! As they parted for the night, they agreed to schedule another date soon.

The next day, George texted Mary to arrange their next date. Mary didn't text back. George waited for a day, then sent Mary a Facebook message. George noticed that Mary saw the message, but she didn't reply. He sent her an email in a couple of days, but Mary maintained radio silence. Eventually, he gave up trying to contact her. *What a disappointment!* George thought. *Just like all those other women. I can't believe I was so wrong about her!*

Why didn't Mary write back? Well, she had a different experience than George on that date. A polite and shy introvert, she felt overwhelmed from the start of the date with George's extroverted and energetic personality. *Why would I date someone who overwhelms me like that?* Mary thought while listening to George talk about his parents, job, and friends without asking her about herself. She politely listened to George, not wanting to hurt his feelings, and told George she'd go out with him again, with absolutely no intention of doing so.

I learned about the widely diverging viewpoints of Mary and George because I knew both of them as casual acquaintances. George started complaining to people around him, including me, about Mary's refusal to respond to his messages after a date that he thought went very well. George felt that he was genuinely sharing and Mary did wonderful listening, while Mary perceived him as oversharing and herself as behaving politely until she could leave. I privately asked Mary what happened from her perspective and she told me her side of the story. Mary told me that she kept sending nonverbal signals of her lack of interest, but George failed to catch the signals.

Now, you might see it as problematic for Mary to avoid responding to George's texts. Still, there are many "Marys" out there who behave this way due to a combination of shyness, politeness, and conflict avoidance in their personality. In turn, there are many "Georges" whose extroversion and energy impede their ability to read nonverbal signals.

Both George and Mary fell into one of the most common judgment errors that cause misunderstandings between us: the "illusion of transparency."[73] This cognitive bias leads to us greatly overestimate the extent to which others perceive our feelings and thoughts. It's one of several biases that cause us to feel, think, and talk past each other, harming our personal, professional, and civic relationships.

Illusion of Transparency

How's your poker face? Do you believe others can tell when you're bluffing? What about when you're straight-out lying: How easy are you to read?

Maybe not as easy as you think. In an experiment where law enforcement officers reviewed ten video tapes of people who either told the truth or lied about their feelings, those from the FBI, CIA, NSA, DEA, and many others failed to detect liars (only the US Secret Service did better than chance).[74] While it's surprisingly hard to detect liars, we also feel overconfident about how well other people read us. Another study separated participants into two groups, with members of the first group answering questions either truthfully or not and the second group guessing whether members of the first lied. About half of those who lied from the first group believed that those from the second group recognized their lies, while in reality only a quarter were caught.[75]

Think you're better at telling who's a liar or not? Do an experiment! Get a couple of your friends together for a lie-off. Tell each other plausible stories about your background that are either true or false, say three of each, and see how many you get right. It's a fun party game! When I tried this with my group of friends, our combined average was around 55 percent at spotting a lie, so just a tiny bit better than choosing randomly. The illusion of transparency is behind the combination of our laughably poor ability to spot lies along with our excessive confidence that we telegraph what we think and feel to others.

The same dangerous judgment error results in negotiators making errors. For instance, studies showed that negotiators who sought to conceal their desires did a better job doing so than they thought they did. In turn, those who tried to convey information to those they negotiated with about their preferences overestimated their abilities to communicate such preferences.[76] A case in point, imagine that you're negotiating with your spouse about whether to spend Thanksgiving with your in-laws. You'd rather not go but don't want to upset your spouse by insisting on not going and are willing to go if your spouse is really determined to spend Thanksgiving there. You might feel you're conveying your nuanced perspective through indirect signals such as nonverbal body language and tone of voice. Chances are, you're not. Your spouse is most likely confused and mistaken about your actual position unless you explicitly and verbally state your perspective.

Don't believe me? Try an experiment: ask your spouse to describe your position on a matter of disagreement that you are negotiating. When Agnes and I tried this after over a decade of marriage, we learned that the indirect signals we thought we read perfectly were wrong 20 to 30 percent of the time. While initially uncomfortable, this knowledge led to us being more transparent and explicit in describing our perspectives on matters of disagreement, as a result significantly improving our relationship.

Many parents will recognize the illusion of transparency from what happens when their children get into their teenage years. In just a few short years, their kids transform from adorable little tykes who sell Girl Scout Cookies and see their mom and dad as the source of all wisdom into argumentative and rebellious teens who stay out late and trust their friends over their parents. What parents miss in the emotional subtext of what their teenagers are saying and doing is that the teens are seeking more autonomy and independence as they enter the world of adulthood and draw closer to their peer groups, which requires distancing from Mom and Dad. What teenagers miss is that their parents want to protect them and keep them safe from the kind of problems the parents themselves experienced growing up.

A greater appreciation of the emotional perspective of each side would address much of the illusion of transparency that causes great drama to parents and children in that life stage. Parents can take the lead in modeling emotional awareness and maturity by, firstly, using empathetic questioning to grasp better the emotional perspective of their children, which also helps the latter become more aware of their feelings. For instance, parents can ask, "Tonya, are you wanting to stay out late because you'd like more control over your life?" That question can lead into a conversation about what it means to have "control" and what's the best balance of autonomy for the teen versus guidance from the parents. Secondly, parents can share their emotions with their teens, empowering the children to understand how their parents truly feel: "Tonya, I'm sorry I snapped at you for coming home so late. I felt anxious about your safety and didn't respond as well as I would have liked." Such comments can help teens understand their parents as human beings with a complex set of emotions, rather than the somewhat one-dimensional view that younger children have of parents as sources of love and authority.

Illusion of Transparency Exercise

The benefits you get from reading this chapter will be illusory if you skip the exercises on the illusion of transparency and other cognitive biases. So please take a few minutes to journal your answers to these questions:

- Where have you fallen into the illusion of transparency in your life? How has doing so harmed your relationships? Where have you seen other people fall for this cognitive bias in their lives? How has doing so harmed their relationships?

Solving the Illusion of Transparency

What if you're being unclear and the other person doesn't get it? What if you're being as clear as possible, but the concept is still too complex for the other person to grasp? What if you're being clear and the other person should get it if they pay attention, but they're distracted for some reason or simply don't care? What if the words used by the parties in a relationship fail to convey the key underlying emotions that explain what's actually going on? Always use *consider alternative explanations* as a critically important method in debiasing the illusion of transparency.

For example, don't assume that the other party in the relationship got your message, either the words themselves or the underlying emotions. Consider the likelihood that you're misreading the other people involved and that they're failing to understand you. Try to overcommunicate in exploring their perspective, needs, and wants and in sharing your own. You're likely to discover many more alternatives and options than you thought possible if you focus only on the key points of disagreement. Even in the areas of disagreement, discuss with each other exactly how important each one is to you, and negotiate a win-win solution where you give to the other side what's important to them.

Thus, you might have told your teenager to be back by midnight, and they might have agreed with your request. You stay up, and they're not back by midnight. You get increasingly anxious, texting them at 12:15, then at 12:25, then calling them at 12:30, all with no response. Finally, they come back home at 12:45. You're by now a nervous wreck and confront them, demanding an explanation for why they're so late and why they didn't call.

Your teen tells you that their phone battery died, so they couldn't keep track of time and had to get a ride from a friend instead of calling Lyft. They tell you to calm down; it's not the end of the world. The teen is feeling defensive and guilty, ready to lash out at you for what they see as your attack on their autonomy and self-control. The confrontation will likely not end well.

What could you as the parent have done to prevent this situation? Well, you could have confirmed that your teen understood the importance of the timing for you. You could have explained your emotions: your desire to balance their right to increased autonomy with your fear and concern about their well-being. Then, you could have asked your teen what they felt about the timeline. Maybe they felt that the timeline was just a suggestion, or perhaps they felt it was unfair and were determined to break it as a way of pushing the limits of your supervision of their behavior. You could also have helped the teen have a deeper understanding of their own emotions and goals by having a broader conversation about this topic using empathetic questioning.

Additionally, you could have discussed what the penalties might be for arriving home late. After all, you being upset is not really a penalty: we're all responsible for our own emotions, and your teen isn't responsible for how you feel. By creating a clear penalty system, perhaps with an escalation of penalties dependent on how late your teen comes home, you can provide your teen with a guidance into the adult world of rights and responsibilities. Moreover, you're not making yourself the "bad guy": the teen has the right to come home late but is responsible for the consequences of their actions. You can bet that the teen will think twice about coming home late—and remember to charge up their phone battery—with such a system. The key to this approach, or any other strategy to address tensions between children and parents, involves fitting any agreement you make to align with the emotional undertones—the needs and wants—of both parties. It doesn't matter what kind of agreements you make: if the incentives of rewards and punishments don't align with the emotions, the agreement won't work out. If you do have such alignment, you will go a long way toward solving the illusion of transparency.

Another vital debiasing strategy to solve the illusion of transparency is to *set a policy for your future self*. The most important policy to set for yourself to address this dangerous judgment error is to take on the responsibility to make sure that when you communicate, the other people both understand your messages thoroughly and also that you truly get what they're saying. Now, such a policy might sound unfair to you. Why should you be accountable? Don't the other people bear any responsibility? How is it just for you to be the adult in the room?

Well, the world, unfortunately, is not fair. Believing otherwise means you're making the dangerous judgment error called the "just-world fallacy," a false expectation that the world is just, with those who do good being rewarded and evildoers punished.[77]

Given that the world is not inherently fair and just, it's up to you to take matters into your own hands if you want to reach your communication goals. That means if you're reading this, and now know about the illusion of transparency and how to fight it, you have to set for your future self the policy of taking accountability for the success of your communication. Otherwise, you are the one responsible for the failure of your relationships due to poor communication since the other person either doesn't know about the illusion of transparency or is not strong enough to overcome the autopilot system's gut reactions.

After you take on the full responsibility for ensuring the effectiveness of the communication in your relationship, the easiest technique to achieve this outcome is to set a policy for your future self of echoing the other person and asking them to echo you. Echoing—also called reflecting—is the simple act of summarizing and paraphrasing in your own words what you perceive the person to have communicated to you. Make sure to echo not simply the content of their message but also the feelings that motivated their message, or at least your best guess at those feelings. For instance, if your teen tells you they want to come home at 1:00 a.m. instead of midnight, with a stubborn and resentful look on their face, you can say something like, "I'm hearing that you'd prefer to come home at 1:00 a.m. and feel upset that I'm restricting your freedom." If you're right in your guess about their emotions, the other party will confirm it; if you're wrong, they will correct you. For instance, your teen might say, "No, I'm not upset that you're restricting my freedom. I'm worried that my friends will make fun of me if I have to leave the party early just to satisfy my parents." Now, you as the parent have much more awareness of what's motivating your teen and can make an informed decision about timing: perhaps let the teen come home late in exchange for texting every thirty minutes from 11:00 p.m. onward confirming they're okay.

Similarly, ask other people to echo you. Thus, ask the teen to echo what you tell them about the timing, and ask them to describe what they think you might be feeling to motivate your words. You'll find yourself developing richer and more meaningful relationships when you do so. Note that while such echoing of emotions is fully appropriate in personal relationships, it might be less appropriate in work and civic relationships, depending on the specific organizational context and interaction. Still, you can try to use nonverbal signals to echo other people's emotions in those settings and enrich and improve your communication that way. For more on echoing and related techniques, check out Marshall Rosenberg's *Nonviolent Communication*.[78]

Solving the Illusion of Transparency Exercise

Please take a few minutes to journal your answers to these questions before going onward:

- How will you use *considering alternative explanations and options* to fight the illusion of transparency? Specifically, how will you implement this strategy? What challenges do you anticipate seeing in this implementation, and how will you overcome these challenges? What metrics will you use to measure your success in implementing this approach? What would the future of your relationships look like if you succeed in your implementation?

- How will you use *setting a policy for your future self* to fight the illusion of transparency? Specifically, how will you implement this strategy? What challenges do you anticipate seeing in this implementation, and how will you overcome these challenges? What metrics will you use to measure your success in implementing this approach? What would the future of your relationships look like if you succeed in your implementation?

Curse of Knowledge

While knowledge is generally good, it carries within it a curse: it's incredibly difficult to remember what it's like to not know what we now know about a topic. We often forget that other people don't know what we know, underestimate the difficulty of learning this information, and fail to teach others effectively. *Curse of knowledge* is the cognitive bias that describes the difficulties in communicating across differences in knowledge.[79]

I remember a friend trying to teach me how to play the drums. "Don't worry, it's easy," he told me when he led me to his drum set. Sitting down, I tried to follow his instructions. He told me to first hit the rack tom and then the brass drum. I had no idea what these were and asked him to explain them to me. He then spent some time explaining what these were and asked me play the drums he indicated, hitting them half a second apart and keeping up the rhythm. I couldn't do it, getting confused quickly. He grew increasingly frustrated, taking over and showing me how to do it, making it look easy. I then tried it, but just couldn't get the movements right, and got more and more frustrated myself over my friend's failure to give me appropriate instructions while he got upset over my failure to learn. It ended up in an argument between us, and we were mad at each other for a couple of weeks after that incident. I was still a young man at the time, not knowing about curse of knowledge. When I learned about this cognitive bias in my PhD program, the incident with my friend immediately came to mind as a perfect illustration of this pattern.

What about you? Did you ever have a friend or family members try to teach you a new skill and push too far too fast? What about you trying to teach someone else a skill and feeling frustrated with their slow learning? The curse of knowledge is likely a major factor in both of these problematic situations.

Curse of Knowledge Exercise

Please take a few minutes to journal your answers to these questions:

- Where have you fallen into the curse of knowledge in your life? How has doing so harmed your relationships? Where have you seen other people fall for this cognitive bias in their lives? How has doing so harmed their relationships?

Solving the Curse of Knowledge

Debiasing the curse of knowledge requires, first and foremost, the method of *considering other people's points of view*. Say you're trying to teach your friend to play the drums, teach your teen how to behave in a job interview and appropriately in the workplace, or teach your romantic partner a foreign language. Don't start by jumping into the thick of teaching the topic. Instead, talk to the other person about why they want to learn the topic so you get a sense of their emotional motivations and level of interest. If your friend feels very determined to make drumming their new hobby and has already purchased a $500 drum set, you'll take one approach; if they just want to know what it feels like to make lots of random musical noise by banging on loud things, you'll need a whole different approach.

You'll be amazed at how many people in the position of teaching others fail to explore the question of motivation. They forget or never learned that emotions explain the large majority of what moves us, not thoughts. Often, the teachers feel enthusiastic about the topic they are teaching and falsely assume that their students feel the same, a dangerous mistake that can undermine effective teaching.

After you learn about what moves them, evaluate their current knowledge. Show your friend your own drum set and welcome them to play, checking out their level of knowledge and natural talent. If they can't hold a steady beat and aren't improving after an hour of guidance from you, perhaps they're not cut out to take up drumming as a hobby.

Then, introduce them to the next smallest possible unit of knowledge and tie it to their existing knowledge in a way that appeals to their motivations. A frequent manifestation of the curse of knowledge involves asking the student to absorb too much information at once, making them feel overwhelmed and frustrated, like the way I felt when my friend tried to teach me drumming. If you understand the other person's motivations and current state of knowledge and aim to provide them with information that satisfied their desires in small and relevant chunks, they will be much more capable of absorbing and integrating it. So if you're teaching someone to play drums and that person already knows how to play the piano, tie your drumming lessons to their baseline knowledge of piano as a percussion instrument.

Solving the Curse of Knowledge Exercise

Please take a few minutes to journal your answers to these questions before going onward:

- How will you use *considering other people's points of view* to fight the curse of knowledge? Specifically, how will you implement this strategy? What challenges do you anticipate seeing in this implementation, and how will you overcome these challenges? What metrics will you use to measure your success in implementing this approach? What would the future of your relationships look like if you succeed in your implementation?

False Consensus Effect

We greatly overestimate the extent to which our friends, family, colleagues, and all other citizens agree with us, creating a sense of a false alignment with them: a cognitive bias called the "false consensus effect."[80]

Think about the last time that a friend expressed an opinion that surprised you. What about a family member? That sense of surprise indicates the false consensus effect in action.

A close friend related to me how she and her husband of over five years started to talk one day about their vision of the future and the world around them. She felt shocked by many things she heard from her husband, and she learned that he had the same experience about some of what she said. They hadn't really talked deeply for a long time, just going about their day-to-day activities and living their lives together. She learned that he grew more materialistic, prioritizing pragmatic material benefits and hedonistic pleasures; by contrast, she focused increasingly on self-awareness and mindfulness, working on personal growth of her heart and mind. Since both were introverted and had separate circles of friends and hobbies, they didn't notice how their perspectives, values, and goals changed over time, causing them to drift apart from each other.

That conversation gravely tested their marriage. They went to couples therapy weekly for more than a year, trying to figure out what to do about their differences. As of today, they are still together, but decided to avoid having children for the next two years while they are figuring out if their marriage will last. That false image of the spouses' visions of the future and the world around them highlights the false consensus effect.

The false consensus effect damages our society as a whole, exacerbating social polarization and causing people to spend more time in polarized communities, according to research.[81] In turn, participation in polarized communities exacerbates the false consensus effect, and online communities encourage greater polarization due to the ability to coordinate more extreme perspectives together.[82] The death penalty, gun regulation, teaching morality in public schools, abortion, defense spending: studies have shown that we greatly overestimate the extent to which other people share our opinions on these and other loaded political topics.[83] Intriguingly, studies show that the false consensus effect extends beyond politics and social issues to relationships with other people and into the relationship with the divine. Study participants generally believe that their personal opinions on important social and ethical issues align with the opinions of God.[84]

False Consensus Effect Exercise

Please take a few minutes to journal your answers to these questions:

- Where have you fallen into the false consensus effect in your life? How has doing so harmed your relationships? Where have you seen other people fall for this cognitive bias in their lives? How has doing so harmed their relationships?

Solving the False Consensus Effect

Do you remember all the times that you felt surprised when your friends, family, professional colleagues, civic or political collaborators, or others with whom you are in a relationship surprised you, especially in a negative way? It's an uncomfortable feeling. It means you were wrong about these people, that your mental model of them was broken. Our autopilot system—the intuitive gut reaction part of our brain—tries to flinch away from that feeling, ignoring it for the sake of retaining our mental model of how we would like those other people to be.

To solve the false consensus effect, we need to take the uncomfortable step of acknowledging this feeling of surprise, using the debiasing strategy of *considering our past experience* to correct the picture in our heads of these people.[85] When I talked to my friend about the situation with her husband, she admitted to me later that after she went to therapy and talked with her husband, she could look back and notice numerous signs that the two of them were drifting apart. However, she hid that information from herself: it was too much to bear, and she didn't want to deal with it, preferring to focus on her daily activities. Her husband fell into the same dangerous pattern of flinching away from the signs he saw as well. Looking back, both recognized they would have been so much better off bringing these facts out into the open and discussing them earlier. Learn from their mistakes rather than suffering by making yours: look back at your past experience in relationships, notice moments of unpleasant surprise, and address them before your relationships suffer a major crisis. It might sound simple, yet it works surprisingly effectively.

Besides looking backward, which is a critically important but reactive response, you can also take the proactive step of looking forward and address the false consensus effect via the debiasing strategy of *making predictions about the future*. How many people do you think will support the death penalty in the next Gallup Poll on this topic? Make a prediction, write it down, and then see whether it matches reality. You can even use this tactic for information you don't currently know but can find out: in this case, "the future" relates to your future knowledge of this question. What do you think the last Gallup Poll on abortion showed about how many people think abortion should be illegal under all circumstances? No, don't Google it, first write down your answer in your journal. Now, take a look at the result. Using such methods, you can improve your ability to address the false consensus effect around social issues. And next time you're at a party and arguing about such topics, suggest everyone do the same thing: write down their prediction and then look it up. You'll be the life of the party! But seriously, this approach is a great way to subtly help others fight the false consensus effect.

Solving the False Consensus Effect Exercise

Please take a few minutes to journal your answers to these questions before going onward:

- How will you use *considering past experiences* to fight the false consensus effect? Specifically, how will you implement this strategy? What challenges do you anticipate seeing in this implementation, and how will you overcome these challenges? What metrics will you use to measure your success in implementing this approach? What would the future of your relationships look like if you succeed in your implementation?

- How will you use *making predictions* to fight the false consensus effect? Specifically, how will you implement this strategy? What challenges do you anticipate seeing in this implementation, and how will you overcome these challenges? What metrics will you use to measure your success in implementing this approach? What would the future of your relationships look like if you succeed in your implementation?

Conclusion

I felt shocked when I first played the game of "lie to me" with my friends, where we each told each other three truths and three lies about ourselves, with the others having to guess the lies. I went into the game with my eyes open, knowing about the research on this topic. Still, my autopilot system was unprepared for the actual reality: I did no better than chance in spotting the lies. Were my friends such good liars? Not at all, they were regular people. It's just that we are terribly bad at telling apart liars from truth-tellers, including the vast majority of law enforcement personnel (except the Secret Service).

With this in mind, I hope you can see the critical role of effective communication for solving the illusion of transparency, the curse of knowledge, and the false consensus effect. The debiasing tools in this chapter will help you do so, and you can gain more techniques on this and other topics on the book's website: http://disasteravoidanceexperts.com/blindspots.

Building on these tools, the next chapter offers insights on the mistakes we make when we underestimate the intensity of emotions, both our own and those of other people, and how to address such empathy failures.

CHAPTER 6

The Importance of Caring

Jasmine couldn't believe it. Tyrone forgot to use the coaster for his coffee again, leaving ugly stains on the beautiful, handmade oak table! It's been nine months since they got married and moved in together, and he still hadn't learned. She told him dozens of times to use a coaster.

Yet that was just the top of the pyramid. She also told him, over and over again, to put his dirty dishes into the dishwasher and leave his dirty socks in the laundry instead of by the bed. He agreed every time, yet in a few days she found him breaking their agreement. He just apologized and said he'd do better next time. But then, he inevitably slipped.

Why did he do it? Was he trying to send her some kind of message? Was he acting out? And even if he didn't do it maliciously, what did he think she was, his maid? His mom? He never listened when she tried to have an adult conversation about the matter, saying it was no big deal and telling her to chill out, promising to remember next time. He just didn't respect her at all! That's it, I'm done with him!

That's what was running through Jasmine's head as she gathered a suitcase, called her best friend asking if she could stay with her while she figured things out. She left a note telling Tyrone he can live like a pig if he wants, but it won't be with her.

When Tyrone came home and found the note, he was shocked. He couldn't believe that Jasmine would leave him over coffee stains, dirty dishes, and laundry. He called his friends, including me, to figure things out and mediate between him and Jasmine, who wasn't returning his calls, which is how I learned about their situation.

Do you think Jasmine was completely wrong, that Tyrone's behavior didn't deserve anything like her response? If so, you might not care much about cleanliness. On the other hand, if you agree with Jasmine's outrage and fully understand how finding a coffee stain for the thirtieth time was the straw that broke the camel's back, you probably have a strong concern for cleanliness. You might be surprised to learn that cleanliness is not a simple matter of personal preference or upbringing. Our genes encode a strong or weak desire for cleanliness.[86] So your personal take on cleanliness stems to a large extent from your DNA.

If you fall on either extreme of the cleanliness spectrum, it's very difficult to understand—on a visceral, emotional, autopilot system level—people on the other end. Some people have a very strong desire for structure and order. Others feel stifled and confined by rules and discipline, desiring spontaneity and freedom.

The differences in their personalities—structured and traditionalist Jasmine and spontaneous and novelty-seeking Tyrone—attracted them to each other as romantic partners. Unfortunately, these same differences made it very hard for them to live together, especially since they failed to figure out and prepare for the clash between their character traits. For Tyrone, the messy behavior represented a nuanced emotional response, with his autopilot system pushing him away subtly from conforming to the structure imposed by Jasmine. Sure, he could have used his intentional system to train himself to notice and change his behavior, but doing so would have required an awareness of the situation and a determination to change it. Unfortunately, his autopilot system simply perceived Jasmine as nagging him about irrelevant topics, and he paid attention to what he perceived as more important things. That's how they ended up separating, and are still trying to work things out.

This chapter focuses on cognitive biases related to evaluating the impact of emotions on oneself and others. We tend to perceive ourselves as primarily moved by logic, not emotions, while in reality, we are much more emotional than logical. That's why, even if Tyrone logically would have liked to follow his wife's guidelines for cleanliness, he failed to do so even without consciously realizing it. We also tend to underestimate greatly the impact of emotions on other people, as shown by Tyrone's shock and disbelief over the extent of Jasmine's reaction to what he perceived as a completely trivial matter, and which she saw as a deal-breaker for her quality of life.

Empathy Gap

We usually underestimate the impact of emotions on other people, as well as on ourselves during times of emotional arousal, a cognitive bias called the "empathy gap."[87] The empathy gap explains many of the more confusing conflicts we have with our loved ones, such as the one between Tyrone and Jasmine. Tyrone was perplexed both by Jasmine's reactions and also by his own behavior, namely by why he had so much trouble following Jasmine's rules of cleanliness. Jasmine, in turn, was confused both by Tyrone's agreement to follow her guidelines and then failure to stick to them as well as the strength of her emotions about his problematic behaviors. It's hard for us to recognize our underlying emotional drivers, especially about things as primal as desire for order or the revulsion response.

For another example of how the empathy gap applies to us, namely the difference between a calm and relaxed state versus an aroused and triggered state, reflect on the last heated argument you had with someone close to you.[88] Did the argument get you what you want? Did you reach your goals in getting the person to either behave or believe the way you would like them to, in a sustainable manner? Or did the argument hurt your relationship, undercutting trust and positive feelings? Most people find that strident arguments harm their relationships while not enabling them to reach their goals. We often regret these arguments when we cool down and frequently don't understand why we said hurtful things in the heat of debate, but the damage is done. The heat of debates results in us getting into an aroused state and relying on our autopilot system's gut reactions, rather than the more deliberative intentional system. That kind of heated debate presents a perfect example of us underestimating the impact of emotions on us: in a cool state, we would never say what we do in heated states.

The empathy gap brings particular harm to relationships in our society as a whole when it combines with tribalism. Due to the horns effect of negative feelings we experience toward people who we perceive as not belonging to our tribe, we have a particularly strong pattern of disregarding the strength of their emotions.[89] This empathy gap rears its ugly head especially toward those who we see as "worse than us" on the privilege hierarchy. That helps explain why people in positions of privilege in any specific domain—gender, sexuality, skin color, religion, and so forth—dismiss as irrelevant the experiences of those who don't share their privilege. The lack of caring for how minorities feel explains many acts of social injustice and discrimination in our society and around the globe. Bridging the empathy gap can heal many social wounds.

Empathy Gap Exercise

You might not feel like you care about doing the exercises, wanting instead to jump ahead and read the next section. WAIT! You're in a hot, excited, emotionally aroused state, and you'll regret the damage your relationships will suffer if you fail to do the exercises as you read this book. So please take out your journal, and spend a few minutes writing down your answers to these questions:

- Where have you fallen into the empathy gap in your life? How has doing so harmed your relationships? Where have you seen other people fall for this cognitive bias in their lives? How has doing so harmed their relationships?

Solving the Empathy Gap

Solving the empathy gap requires drawing on the debiasing strategy of *considering other people's points of view*. Try to think about how you would feel about the situation in their shoes and if you had their background. For example, take the example of tribalism and privilege, and try to take the perspective of those with privilege and without. Reflect on an area of your life where you lack privilege: ethnicity, gender, religion, sexuality, ability, cultural background, or other. Take me as a case study. I live with a mental illness, and I have a Slavic accent, both of which are unfortunately looked down upon in the United States. Using these areas where I lack privilege, I can try to bridge mentally the empathy gap toward other areas where I am in a position of privilege, such as being a white male, and empathize with those who do not have such privilege. You can do the same mental bridging.

Of course, different types of privilege work differently in our society. For example, the internal experience of being a Muslim and suffering Islamophobia is quite distinct from being poor, and the internal experience of suffering discrimination from being an immigrant with a Slavic accent differs from the racism suffered by African Americans. Still, there is a commonality shared across all forms of being lower down on the societal hierarchy, and you can capture at least some aspects of this experience if you try.

A useful tactic for helping get other people's emotional perspectives involves listening empathetically and echoing to confirm you understood. In empathetic listening, you focus less on the content of the other person's words than on figuring out what feelings motivate their words. For example, when I conducted focus groups and one-on-one interviews with the software engineers, I paid most of my attention to how excited they seemed about various aspects of their job, along with what people they respected as role models and whose approval they sought. Focusing on these helped me understand how they truly felt and what really motivated and engaged them, regardless of whether they paid lip service to the company's officially stated guidelines. Similarly, when I talked to Tyrone, I could see that he paid lip service to the importance of cleanliness but would have been happier in a much less strict environment. Subtle echoing—using the techniques discussed in the previous chapter—helped confirm both the feelings of the software engineers and Tyrone.

These conversations don't need to take a long time. A fascinating study on reducing prejudice against transgender people in South Florida had canvassers go door-to-door and hold ten-minute dialogues focused on having the people they spoke with consider the perspective of transgendered individuals. Specifically, the canvassers asked those who answered the door and agreed to speak to recall a time when they felt judged due to being different. Next, the canvasser asked the person to see how their experience being judged illuminated an aspect of the kind of daily experiences suffered by transgendered individuals. The canvassers then asked the person about the impact of the exercise. The study showed that such brief conversations significantly reduced transphobia and increased support for an anti-discrimination law, with the effect of the conversation lasting for at least three months.[90] Given the strong transphobia in the US, we can safely assume that the perspective-taking exercise in the study would work on other forms of discrimination. If you have any leadership influence in a civic or social group, that might be a good fit for such an exercise; try it!

The debiasing approach of *making predictions about the future* also offers a great way to address the empathy gap, and the situation with Tyrone and Jasmine offers a perfect example. If you knew in advance that your romantic partner cared a lot about order—say, planning out every aspect of your date—and had a strong disinclination to have new experiences, you could predict that they would care a lot about cleanliness. Anticipating their strong emotions when you're in a rational and cool state, as opposed to an emotional arousal caused by a fight about cleanliness, will help you make a wise and well-informed decision about your path forward. If you're not so concerned about cleanliness yourself, are you willing to live with someone who's a disciplinarian about it? If not, perhaps you should consider not living together.

Solving the Empathy Gap Exercise

Please take a few minutes to journal your answers to these questions before going onward:

- How will you use *considering other people's points of view* to fight the empathy gap? Specifically, how will you implement this strategy? What challenges do you anticipate seeing in this implementation, and how will you overcome these challenges? What metrics will you use to measure your success in implementing this approach? What would the future of your relationships look like if you succeed in your implementation?

- How will you use *making predictions about the future* to fight the empathy gap? Specifically, how will you implement this strategy? What challenges do you anticipate seeing in this implementation, and how will you overcome these challenges? What metrics will you use to measure your success in implementing this approach? What would the future of your relationships look like if you succeed in your implementation?

Bystander Effect

How much do you care if a stranger is in trouble? Would you help them in an emergency? Let's say you're coming back from an important business meeting, dressed in your nicest attire. You're passing by a pond, and suddenly, you hear a scream. You see a child standing by the edge of the pond, and another one deep in the pond, clearly struggling. Would you jump into the pond and ruin your best and most expensive business clothing to save the child?

Now imagine you're walking from the same business meeting, but with a group of colleagues. You all see the child drowning. Would you jump in to save the child or wait for someone else to do so? After all, you don't want to ruin your suit, and it would be pretty socially awkward to try to save the child in front of your colleagues. And hey, maybe the child is playing around, maybe it's not a big deal. How embarrassed would you feel?

Next, imagine you find out that there's an organization dedicated to saving drowning children. You're convinced it's very effective. How much money would you donate to the organization to save drowning children?[91]

Due to the faulty wiring in our minds, we are much more willing to help people in a critical situation if we are the only one available to help. The more people that witness an emergency and are available to help, the less likely we are to help, and instead stand by while the emergency plays out, a cognitive bias called the "bystander effect."[92]

The same problem occurs in personal relationships. If someone has many friends, you'd expect that they would get a lot of help if their friends learn that they're in trouble, especially if the person makes a public post about it on Facebook or sends out a mass email. Likewise, you'd have the same expectation for someone in a challenging situation in their job who posts a message on LinkedIn. Unfortunately, our gut reactions cause us to feel much less concerned and thus less likely to help in such cases.

While we're not sure of all the reasons for the bystander effect, we know that two major reasons stem from diffusion of responsibility and social signaling. Regarding the former, if we are the only ones who can help, we feel much more responsible for the outcome of the situation, greatly increasing our likelihood of helping out. The more people who may potentially help, the more responsibility diffuses across all of them. As a result, if helping takes a significant cost, such as ruining a $1,500 suit to save a drowning child, with enough people around, responsibility may become so diffused that no one is willing to pay the cost because no one feels the burden of responsibility.

Social signaling offers a serious obstacle to responding to emergencies or broad requests for help because of how much our behavior relies on observing others around us. If there are many people around and due to the diffusion of responsibility, none of them behaves as though the situation is an emergency, then we will be less likely to perceive it as an emergency as well. The reluctance to behave in a socially awkward manner that breaks social norms, causing other people to judge us negative and reject us, poses a very powerful inhibitor to our autopilot system.

Bystander Effect Exercise

Take out your journal, and spend a few minutes writing down your answers to these questions:

- Where have you fallen into the bystander effect in your life? How has doing so harmed your relationships? Where have you seen other people fall for this cognitive bias in their lives? How has doing so harmed their relationships?

Solving the Bystander Effect

Addressing the bystander effect in others is relatively easy, and this one takeaway from the book may save your life or the life of a loved one in an emergency. Say you're the victim of an emergency, or want to help the victim, and are surrounded by a bunch of bystanders. What you need to do is break through the diffusion of responsibility and social signaling.[93] Don't simply yell out, "Help me!" That phrase diffuses the responsibility. Instead, point to a specific person and give specific directions: say, "You, woman in the blue sweater, call 911," and "You, guy with the bike, ride down to the Walgreens pharmacy five blocks down the street and get some gauze pads and hydrogen peroxide."

If you're in trouble and need some help from your friends, don't simply post about your problems it on Facebook or LinkedIn. Instead, decide on what kind of concrete aid you need and who in particular might provide it. Then, send them private messages asking them to help you. Depending on the situation, you can ask a close friend to organize help for you.

For instance, my wife Agnes knew about the bystander effect and offered to help a close friend organize a support network during her pregnancy. Coordinating with the friend, Agnes asked specific people for various forms of help, ranging from cooking and bringing over meals to watching the baby (I helped out with yardwork, being neither a good cook nor competent with babies). With such support, the friend had a much less stressful first year after childbirth.

Set a clear policy for your future self as another powerful debiasing strategy for the bystander effect. Once I learned about this cognitive bias, I decided on an internal policy for my future self of not waiting for other people around me to act when I see what appears to be an emergency. Since the bystander effect will cause all of us to be less likely to act than is appropriate for the situation, I made a decision to—regardless of other people's behaviors—rush to call 911 or dive in to save a drowning child from a pond. It's better for 911 to get two calls or for two people to ruin their fancy clothing rather than delaying the help that's needed and potentially threatening the life of a child.

Solving the Bystander Effect Exercise

Please take a few minutes to journal your answers to these questions before going onward:

- How will you use *setting a clear policy for your future self* to address the bystander effect? Specifically, how will you implement this strategy? What challenges do you anticipate seeing in this implementation, and how will you overcome these challenges? What metrics will you use to measure your success in implementing this approach? What would the future of your relationships look like if you succeed in your implementation?

Conclusion

It's extremely easy to underestimate the strength and nature of other people's emotions as well as of our own feelings between cool and hot states. It's not that Tyrone deliberately and maliciously left stains, dishes, and laundry for Jasmine to clean up. He simply did not grasp the true importance of cleanliness to Jasmine and perceived her as nagging when she brought up these matters. Moreover, due to his own preference for spontaneity, Tyrone's own autopilot system caused him to flinch away from the growing signs of Jasmine's real feelings. Similarly, Jasmine didn't get how Tyrone felt. Without an understanding of the empathy gap, and debiasing tools to address this dangerous judgment error, their relationship had little chance.

The same empathy gap undermines our ability to keep our cool and have effective conversations on topics of disagreement, resulting in arguments that we later regret. The related problem of bystander effect reduces our caring, both feelings and behaviors, about troubles suffered by other people, strangers and friends.

Fortunately, there's cause for optimism, as the debiasing tactics in this chapter empower you to address the dangerous gut reactions that harm our miscalibration of emotions within ourselves and others. For more techniques, visit this book's website: http://disasteravoidanceexperts.com/blindspots.

The next chapter addresses another kind of miscalibration from which most of us suffer, namely in assessing risks and rewards, with a focus on optimism and pessimism.

CHAPTER 7

The Glass Is Half...

My wife Agnes having a nervous breakdown in July 2014 was the time of the biggest strain on our marriage, but it wasn't the time when we had the most conflicts. Neither did she and I have the most conflicts in our marriage in late 2003, the year we had our wedding and moved in together, despite us having to learn to live with each other. In fact, we had the most conflicts in our marriage a decade after our wedding, in February and March 2014, when we co-founded a nonprofit, Intentional Insights, dedicated to popularizing research on cognitive biases and wise decision-making strategies.

Previously, Agnes and I collaborated on many household projects, but never on anything as big as founding a nonprofit. Immediately, we started having many conflicts about the strategy of this organization.

Here's my experience of these conflicts: Whenever I was struck by inspiration and shared an idea about how to move forward with an aspect of the nonprofit, excited and enthusiastic about the potential of this initiative, she would get a concerned look on her face. She would start to criticize the idea, pointing out the many ways it could go wrong. We would then argue, me pointing out all the good aspects of the idea, while she focused on the flaws. We would eventually compromise on how to move forward in a specific area, a settlement that usually didn't satisfy either of us, leaving us both feeling disturbed and displeased.

I left those early strategy meetings exhausted and disconnected. She did as well. They weren't healthy for our personal relationship. We grew more distant and had to put in a lot of hard work to maintain our previous level of emotional connection.

Did you ever experience such conflicts? Do you have someone in your life who criticizes good ideas that you offer? It happens frequently within families, when someone proposes a major project, such as remodeling the house or a family vacation. It happens within civic institutions, such as clubs or value-based groups, when someone proposes an innovative initiative. In my consulting with businesses and nonprofits, I've seen such criticism be a major cause of team conflict, with some team members coming up with many ideas while others simply shoot down these ideas.

Why do these people do so? Well, later when Agnes and I figured out and resolved the root of the problem, we understood what occurred. See if you can spot what happened.

From her perspective, I was being reckless. She saw me as sharing half-baked ideas that might harm the organization's long-term future. She didn't see me offering ways of implementing much of what I came up with and thus saw the ideas as impractical and dangerous. Anxious about the damage that could be done through taking unwarranted risks, she perceived herself as having no choice but to argue against these ideas and protect the nonprofit.

Do you have anyone in your life, community, or workplace who regularly shares half-baked ideas? Do you feel yourself obliged to stand up and push back against these impractical initiatives? Then you understand the place from which Agnes came.

What you might have realized by now—and what Agnes and I eventually came to see—was that the two of us had a critically important personality difference in how we approached risk and reward. I tend to be optimistic, meaning I have a gut feeling that everything will go well in the future, inclining me to be excessively risk-blind; she tends to be pessimistic, perceiving dangers in the future, causing her to be too risk-averse. I see the glass as half full, and she sees it as half empty; I see grass as always green on the other side of the hill, and she sees the grass as yellow.

Optimists like me usually generate many ideas about what to do since they have a risk-blind vision of a bright future. They share the broad outlines of these ideas with others without thoroughly thinking through the implementation details or the practicalities of all aspects of these ideas. By contrast, pessimists generally create much fewer ideas because they intuitively see the future as dark and focus their attention on the flaws of any idea they create. Moreover, pessimists usually avoid sharing ideas until they reflected on how to enact them in real life.

So if you are an idea person and others shoot down your ideas, you're likely an optimist. If you're the person who has to keep others' feet on the ground when their heads go into the sky, you're probably a pessimist. Neither is better or worse: both represent a flawed form of thinking.

Unfortunately, either type of flawed thinking hurts you when you make mistakes because of taking too many or too few risks, and these mistakes—to the extent they impact others—can seriously damage your relationships. Moreover, if you're collaborating with people who have the opposite approach to risk and reward, you'll likely end up butting heads a lot and undermining your relationships, unless you use the kind of effective collaborative decision-making strategies that Agnes and I ended up using and that we both later brought into our consulting work with our clients. This chapter will shed more light on problems resulting from excessive risk-blindness and risk-aversion and also provide the tools to address these issues in your personal relationships, civic life, and professional activities.

Optimism Bias

"Optimism bias" refers to the cognitive bias of underestimating the likelihood of negative future events.[94] From an evolutionary psychology perspective, it's beneficial for some members of a tribe to feel overconfident about a bright future.[95] These people would be more willing to take risks, going out and exploring to find new resources. Likewise, optimism bias encourages young males to fight other tribes in situations when resources are contested: if the tribe's warriors did not have an inflated estimate of their survival in battle, the tribe might not survive. Furthermore, an optimistic individual would be more likely to struggle for higher social status within the tribe, making that person more likely to reproduce and pass on their genes if they win. Optimists try to do many more things and as a result fail much more often than pessimists, which in the savanna environment often equated to death; yet, when they succeeded, they tended to reproduce more often than pessimists, helping explain why about 80 percent of us—across race, ethnicity, and gender lines—have an optimism bias.[96]

Yet that's not the only reason for the widespread nature of excessive optimism. The optimism bias seems to have a number of benefits.[97] For instance, it seems to help decrease depression and anxiety, improve health and longevity, and increase productivity.

Of course, such benefits come with serious dangers, such as a greater likelihood of harmful behaviors, such as smoking, excessive spending, and obesity, due to unrealistic assumptions about avoiding the costs of such behaviors. Likewise, economists attribute the boom-and-bust cycle of financial bubbles, such as the

2008 Great Recession, to society-wide optimism. About a fifth of all small businesses fail within a year of opening their doors, and half of all small businesses fail within the first five years.[98] Political leaders can make terrible decisions under the influence of optimism, such as wrongly assuming that an armed intervention into a foreign country will be well-received by the population there. Recent revelations have shown how religious leaders made horrendous decisions to cover up abuses of children, assigning too low a probability to the likelihood that these abuses will be uncovered.

The danger of the optimism bias to relationships stems both from conflicts with the pessimists in your life—such as the relationship between me and Agnes—as well as from bad decisions that damage your relationships with others. A case in point: Chen is an inveterate optimist. He's a great cook, inspired by his grandma's recipes of Chinese food and his own imagination to make Chinese fusion dishes. He often hosts friends at his house, and they express delight over his creative cooking.

Having worked as a software engineer for over a decade, he was laid off when his company merged with another. He decided to use this lemon handed to him to make lemonade by opening a Chinese fusion restaurant called Grandma and Me.

To get the initial starting capital, Chen tried to get approval for a bank loan of $125,000. Unfortunately, due to the high failure rate of small businesses, he didn't get the money he needed. Instead, he decided to borrow the money from the friends he invited to his house, promising to pay them back with significant interest in a year, after his new establishment took off. Enthusiastic over his cooking and trusting that other people will love it as well, they ponied up the money.

Chen launched the restaurant to great fanfare, with all his friends—most of them debtees—in attendance. They spread word to their friends, and some came. However, the food proved too unusual, not matching their expectations. When cooking in his home, Chen explained all aspects of the meal, entertaining and captivating his audience while they ate. Chen's stories and enthusiasm made a huge difference to the enjoyment of their experience, helping them overcome the out-of-the-box nature of the food. In the restaurant, Chen had to spend his time cooking instead. As a result, after the first burst of enthusiasm, negative reviews started to add up on Google and Yelp. Fewer and fewer people came to the restaurant.

Chen, a great cook and solid programmer, lacked skills in marketing and sales and didn't take the time to learn them before launching his restaurant. Neither did he evaluate the likelihood of failure, considering the probabilities involved. He didn't even make a solid business plan, riding the high of enthusiasm from his friends combined with his optimism.

Blind to the risks of starting this business, he would up owing a lot of money to his friends. While they liked his food, once they found out that he didn't take the time to educate himself on how to be a business owner, the large majority felt very upset with Chen. He didn't have the means to pay them back. Unsurprisingly— given that money represents one of the biggest sources of conflict in relationships—many turned away from Chen.

Chen's blind belief that the quality of his cooking and failure both to realize the critical role of his storytelling in easing people into his unusual food and, even more importantly, to plan ahead for potential problems with his business, exemplifies the flawed thinking that brings down optimists and decimates their relationships. They tend to overestimate their own capacities, perceive other people as more friendly and supportive than they are, and ignore potential pitfalls in their plans.

Optimism Bias Exercise

You might feel confident about your ability to deal with the optimism bias without doing the exercises. Well, hate to throw a bucket of cold water over your confidence, but you're likely too optimistic, like 80 percent of the population. Don't let your gut intuitions lead you astray. Instead, please take out your journal, and spend a few minutes writing down your answers to these questions:

- Where have you fallen into the *optimism bias* in your life? How has doing so harmed your relationships? Where have you seen other people fall for this cognitive bias in their lives? How has doing so harmed their relationships?

Solving Optimism Bias

How did Agnes and I solve our conflicts? You might suspect that we decided to compromise, settling each question by deciding to somewhere halfway between my optimism and her pessimism. You'd be wrong.

Now, make no mistake, compromise holds a vital place in a close relationship, romantic or otherwise. Agnes and I compromise often when we have different preferences. I prefer the temperature in the house to be at 75, she prefers it at 69, so we set it at 72. I prefer sit-down restaurants, she prefers counter service, so we take turns going first to one and then another for our weekly date nights. Such compromises reflect our different values and tastes and represent part of the give-and-take of a healthy marriage.

However, with the nonprofit, we both had the same value: using our resources to spread knowledge about cognitive biases and science-based decision making as widely as possible. Our disagreement wasn't on values, but on methods. While we can't objectively say that "69 is better" or "75 is better," we can evaluate whether a specific method offers a more or less effective way of achieving our shared values of advancing the mission.

So instead of compromising, we collaborated. Each of us played to our strengths, using the debiasing strategy of *getting an external perspective* from each other.

When we discussed strategy, I would come up with a bunch of ideas. Then, I'd distance myself from ownership of these half-baked ideas and give them to Agnes. She would select a couple of those ideas that she perceived as having the least flaws—in terms of getting the biggest potential output from our resource investment—and then discard the rest. Then, she would finish baking the ideas by pointing out their potential flaws and working with me to generate ways to address the flaws. As a result of this collaboration between me, as an optimist, and her, as a pessimist, we would get some masterfully baked ideas that had a powerful impact with minimal resource investment. We now use similar strategies to mediate conflicts between optimists and pessimists among our friends, in our communities, and in our work life.

A related debiasing strategy involves *making a precommitment* to inform others in your life about your optimism bias and asking them to remind you about your excessively bright vision of the future when you get too excited. Both Agnes and I tell about our personal predilections to others to help them rein us in and also to help those people make better assessments of our judgments.

Chen would have benefitted greatly both from getting an external perspective from more pessimistically oriented friends and especially from telling others about his optimism. If others knew he tended to be too optimistic, they would have encouraged him to spend more time evaluating his business plans before opening up his restaurant. Likewise, they would have been much less likely to lend him the money. Even if they did make the loan, they would have done so with the knowledge of his tendency to have inflated estimates of his own capacities and have been much more ready to lose the money, minimizing consequent damage to their relationships with Chen.

Solving the Optimism Bias Exercise

Please take a few minutes to journal your answers to these questions before going onward:

- How will you use *getting an external perspective* to fight the optimism bias? Specifically, how will you implement this strategy? What challenges do you anticipate seeing in this implementation, and how will you overcome these challenges? What metrics will you use to measure your success in implementing this approach? What would the future of your relationships look like if you succeed in your implementation?

- How will you use *making a precommitment* to get others around you to support your efforts to address your optimism bias? Specifically, how will you implement this strategy? What challenges do you anticipate seeing in this implementation, and how will you overcome these challenges? What metrics will you use to measure your success in implementing this approach? What would the future of your relationships look like if you succeed in your implementation?

Pessimism Bias

"Pessimism bias," unsurprisingly, is the cognitive bias of overestimating future dangers.[99] It's much less prevalent than the optimism bias, so you should especially treasure the rare people in your life who can prove a more skeptical look at the future.

Just like it makes evolutionary sense for some members of a tribe to have excessively positive views of the future, the same is true for pessimism.[100] Risk-averse tribe members stayed behind and let the optimists explore and find resources: pessimists instead conserved resources. So in tough times, pessimists would tend to help the tribe more, while in good times optimists would bring more benefits to the tribe.

For the individual, pessimism tends to be less healthy than optimism. Pessimists tend to suffer from depression more often.[101] They also have worse physical health outcomes.[102] Moreover, in American society, pessimism is often looked down upon, resulting in an unfortunate stigma against pessimists as naysayers or Debbie Downers, making it harder for them to form healthy social bonds.[103] Yet pessimism, as research shows, can be quite beneficial for self-reflection and progress.[104] Likewise, pessimism offers substantial benefits for coping with risky situations.[105]

People started calling Charlotte a Debbie Downer soon after a popular Saturday Night Live sketch in 2004 associated this phrase with a person who makes negative comments and brings others down. Charlotte grew sick of the phrase, but she couldn't help her intuitive urges to help people see the dangers in their excessively positive outlooks. She felt appalled that those around her—family, friends, members of her church, and coworkers—always seemed to adopt the motto of Monty Python's 1979 song "Always Look on the Bright Side of Life." They usually ignored her warnings and cautions, despite the fact that they often turned out true. She felt like a modern-day Cassandra, the figure from Greek mythology who told true prophecies that were not believed.

What Charlotte didn't realize was that when she criticized other people's plans and projects, they felt attacked as people. She made comments such as, "Buying that luxury car is a dumb idea," to her friends; "That bake sale fundraiser will never work," to her fellow church members; and "We'll never land that account," to her work colleagues. She didn't recognize that intuitively, pessimists like herself perceive such criticism as a means of supporting and helping others; yet to most people—both optimists and pessimists—critical comments phrased in this way come off as attacks. Such destructive criticism—rather than the kind of constructive criticism that Agnes learned to do in improving ideas after we figured out how to collaborate well together—did not sit well with others. Charlotte had trouble making friends; she had few allies either in her church or her work.

Charlotte used the same sort of destructive criticism toward herself, in her mental self-talk. She didn't like being slightly overweight, and self-directed thoughts like *fatso* passed through her mind whenever she looked in a mirror. Any time she suffered a work setback, her mind went to a dark place. Whenever she had a minor conflict with a friend, she ruminated on it for days, envisioning the friend leaving her.

Pessimism Bias Exercise

Please take out your journal, and spend a few minutes writing down your answers to these questions:

- Where have you fallen into the *pessimism bias* in your life? How has doing so harmed your relationships? Where have you seen other people fall for this cognitive bias in their lives? How has doing so harmed their relationships?

Solving the Pessimism Bias

Getting an external perspective and *making precommitments* work not only for the optimism bias, but also for the pessimism bias. Agnes uses the first to improve greatly her collaboration with me and uses the second to get others around her to assist her in reevaluating her plans. However, pessimists usually have less social support than optimists, both due to the stigma against pessimists in our society as well as due to the difficulty that pessimists have with maintaining strong social bonds and providing social support in the way that other people want.

It really helps pessimists to use the debiasing strategy of *considering other people's points of view*. Remember that most people are optimists and don't see problems with their plans and ideas. Destructive criticism of the sort leveled by Charlotte—where the criticism simply attacks what others put forward—will generally provoke a defensive fight-or-flight response. The person criticized will either shut down and be quiet, which is a form of flight, or will argue back without considering the validity of the criticism, resulting in a heated and destructive debate.

A much more effective way for pessimists to support others—which Agnes learned and which we now teach others—involves identifying specific areas that can be made better. It's even better to put forth concrete suggestions for improvement. Such criticism is constructive instead of destructive, meaning it helps build up both the idea and, even more important, the relationship with the person whose notion you're critiquing. You are putting yourself on the same side as them, conveying emotionally that you share their goals of making the idea work and are enthusiastic about helping make sure it does so through focusing on what should be improved.

So instead of saying, "Buying that luxury car is a dumb idea," to your friend, say something like, "Great to hear that you're thinking about that. Can you help me understand how that purchase will advance your goal of early retirement?" Instead of saying, "That bake sale fundraiser will never work," say something like, "I'm crossing my fingers that a bake sale fundraiser will raise the money we need to fix the roof. Just in case it doesn't quite make it, what other fundraisers can we run?" Instead of, "We'll never land that account," tell your coworkers, "That's a great stretch goal, and we should go for it. In case we don't make it, what are some lower-hanging fruits we should target to meet our quarterly sales goals?"

That same strategy will also help you with self-talk. Consider what constructive criticism you'd use to talk to a friend. Instead of *fatso*, perhaps you can say something like, *I'd prefer to lose a little weight. Perhaps it would help to start biking to work instead of driving?* When you suffer a work setback, focus on what you can learn and how you can improve going forward. When you have a minor conflict with a friend and imagine the friend will leave you, recognize that if the friend is the type of person to leave over a minor conflict, they're not a good person for you anyway.

If you still have trouble with ruminations and negative self-talk, consider getting professional help. Charlotte ended up doing so and was diagnosed with depression. After three months going to a CBT-style therapist, she felt much better, and her self-talk grew much more constructive.

Solving the Pessimism Bias Exercise

Please take a few minutes to journal your answers to these questions before going onward:

- How will you use *getting an external perspective* to fight the pessimism bias? Specifically, how will you implement this strategy? What challenges do you anticipate seeing in this implementation, and how will you overcome these challenges? What metrics will you use to measure your success in implementing this approach? What would the future of your relationships look like if you succeed in your implementation?

- How will you use *making a precommitment* to get others around you to support your efforts to address your pessimism bias? Specifically, how will you implement this strategy? What challenges do you anticipate seeing in this implementation, and how will you overcome these challenges? What metrics will you use to measure your success in implementing this approach? What would the future of your relationships look like if you succeed in your implementation?

- How will you use *considering other people's points of view* to help yourself address your pessimism bias? Specifically, how will you implement this strategy? What challenges do you anticipate seeing in this implementation, and how will you overcome these challenges? What metrics will you use to measure your success in implementing this approach? What would the future of your relationships look like if you succeed in your implementation?

Conclusion

After Agnes and I learned how to turn our respective pessimism and optimism biases from a source of conflict and weakness into a true strength via the strategy of getting an external perspective from each other, we started applying this strategy to our civic activism and our professional work. I would tell Agnes the details of my consulting business projects, which focused on leadership, teamwork, and employee motivation, and I ran my plans by her for help in correcting potential flaws resulting from my optimism.

She, in turn, would tell me more about the details of her consulting business: she specializes in improving nonprofit systems, processes, and organization. My help involved providing her with innovative, out-of-the-box ideas on addressing unusual client issues.

Eventually, we learned to work together so well that after she recovered from her nervous breakdown, we merged our consulting businesses into one. We are now business partners, and our marriage is thriving, along with our professional and civic collaborations. If you had told me she and I would be spending our work-life together in March 2014, I would have laughed in your face, but here we are. What we've learned is that the key is to acknowledge your own bias and work to address it while taking advantage of its strengths: be a realistic optimist or a realistic pessimist. For more on our experience, and other relevant debiasing techniques and stories, make sure to visit this book's website: http://disasteravoidanceexperts.com/blindspots.

It might be tempting to avoid integrating these tactics or doing the exercises. You'll be interested to learn that such reactions might indicate that you're prone to one of the biases described in the next chapter, namely a reluctance to listen to others even when they share ideas that will help you.

CHAPTER 8

(Don't) Tell Me What to Do!

I was the best man at the wedding of my very close friend Jeff. Yet less than a year before the wedding, Jeff didn't want to get married to his long-time girlfriend, despite her desire for them to get married.[106]

Jeff always held a negative attitude toward marriage. He saw it as something imposed by society to enforce morality and restrict sexuality. The legalistic aspect of marriage, from his perspective, went against the attitude of trust and emotional bonding with his girlfriend. He believed it hypocritical to make a life-long promise, when in reality so many marriages end in divorce.

Yet with the political upheaval associated with the 2016 presidential election, Jeff decided to reevaluate some of his personal choices. As he told me, "I have to start making better, more responsible choices than ever before." As part of this reevaluation, he took a long, hard look at how he thought about marriage.

He realized that the underlying cause of his objection to marriage stemmed from his desire to avoid giving in to social and peer pressure. As a nonconformist, he did not wish to bow down to mainstream relationship institutions. He really related to Marlon Brando's movie character as a 1950s motorcycle-gang leader in *The Wild One*, who replied to the question, "What are you rebelling against?" with, "Whadda you got?" as well as Zach de la Rocha of the rock band Rage Against the Machine, screaming, "*F*** YOU, I WON'T DO WHAT YOU TELL ME!*" Jeff said, "If I feel that society expects me to do a thing, I tend to not want to do it, or to want to do the opposite."

When he thought more about his automatic nonconformism, he recognized that this feeling did not serve him well in some instances, including in the most important relationship in his life. After all, as he recognized, getting married would get him and his girlfriend many benefits. On the social network front, he would get support from his girlfriend's family and friends, and his girlfriend would get the same from his. From a legal standpoint, they would be connected to the social security system, gain the chance for joint health insurance, and have various recognitions from the law, such as medical decision-making power and automatic next-of-kin standing for inheritance.

All of these outweighed the discomfort he felt around marriage, once he looked at them using his intentional system, as opposed to just letting his autopilot system steer him away from conforming to social norms. He proposed, and she accepted. Jeff felt relieved, as though some part of him always knew that marrying his girlfriend was the right choice; he also felt proud of not being held back by the obstacle of automatic nonconformism.

While being nonconformist on autopilot can harm your relationships, so can automatic conformism. This chapter looks at both of these problems and provides strategies for addressing these problems.

Reactance

Scholars call what Jeff experienced "reactance," the cognitive bias of feeling negative emotions when someone or something limits one's freedom of behavior or range of choices.[107] People prone to this bias experience it automatically whether the limitation affects them or not.

Reactance has a clear evolutionary explanation in the tribal savanna environment. First, it helped the tribe to have some members who did not conform to the mainstream. Such individuals questioned bad leadership decisions, providing opportunities to evaluate more thoroughly and change the decisions before implementation. Questioning mainstream trends also empowers innovation, which results in improving existing ways of doing things as well as adapting to changes in the environment. Second, a stronger reactance response in the life cycle stage when children matured into adulthood helped teenagers separate from their parents and find their own role in the tribe.

The latter reaction response, tied to hormonal changes in the brain, has just as much relevance now as it did then. A case in point, consider Sally and her fifteen-year-old daughter Lizzy.

Sally didn't like Lizzy's new boyfriend, Mark. Lizzy always had good grades and regularly made the honor roll. Mark, by contrast, usually got Cs and Ds. Lizzy dressed well, while Mark generally went around disheveled. Lizzy spent time after school volunteering and doing yoga while Mark played video games.

Sally felt worried about Mark's influence on Lizzy. After several weeks, she couldn't hold it in much longer and confronted Lizzy about Mark. In the past, Lizzy listened to her mother's evaluations of people, but not this time. Lizzy defended Mark as a kind and compassionate guy, a sensitive and free soul who's misunderstood by Sally and the rest of the world. It was the first time that Lizzy raised her voice at Sally, declaring that she loved Mark and asking her mother to leave him alone.

What Sally didn't know is that Lizzy harbored her own doubts about Mark. She found him intriguing because of his difference from her. He proudly referred to himself as a slacker and so did his friends. Brought up by Sally as ambitious and driven, Lizzy appreciated the sense of peace and comfort provided by Mark and his peers as a way to escape the pressure at home.

Still, Lizzy found it hard to relate to Mark. He didn't seem interested in anything outside video games, hanging out, and sex. He felt content to stay in their small town after finishing high school, while Lizzy was already planning which colleges she might attend.

However, Sally's attack on Mark felt like even more pressure to Lizzy to stay on the straight-and-narrow path of the life that her mom wanted her to lead. Lizzy put aside her doubts about Mark, standing up for him and leading into her first major conflict with her mom. She proceeded to date him for a few more months, fighting with her mom in the meanwhile. Her relations with her mom grew frosty, while her dad wisely held back from the fray. Eventually, her dad prevailed on her mom to tamper down her negative feelings and accept her daughter's romantic choice. Sally stopped making biting comments about Mark, and her relationship with her daughter gradually improved. A few weeks after Sally stopped her war against Mark, Lizzy broke up with him.

While Jeff's reactance stems from his core personality, Lizzy's reactance comes from the specific life cycle stage of teenagers freeing themselves from the influence of their parents and seeking autonomy. Sally clearly miscalculated in using her standard techniques, which worked previously, to try to get Lizzy to stop dating Mark. Sally's autopilot system did what felt comfortable and familiar, and her mistake represents an error frequently made by parents: using the same parenting methods on teens as they used when their children were younger. Unfortunately, going on autopilot and assuming the same methods would work is a big mistake due to the changes in the teenage brain stemming from hormonal dynamics.[108] Another important change is the shifting social climate where peer groups assume increasing importance in driving behaviors.[109] It's critical for parents to use their intentional system to alter how they parent their children during the transition into the teenage years to avoid the kind of harmful conflict and negative outcomes that both Sally and Lizzy suffered.

Reactance Exercise

"I won't do what you tell me"—you might be feeling that when I suggest you do the reactance exercise. I hope you won't let this harmful gut reaction lead you astray from the important role played by these exercises in helping you address cognitive biases for the sake of improving your relationships. Instead, please take out your journal, and spend a few minutes writing down your answers to these questions:

- Where have you fallen into *reactance* in your life? How has doing so harmed your relationships? Where have you seen other people fall for this cognitive bias in their lives? How has doing so harmed their relationships?

Solving Reactance

In dealing with reactance, we need to consider two types of situations. In one situation, you are the one experiencing reactance due to someone else limiting your freedom and options, and you'd like to make the best decisions for your relationships in spite of that automatic reactance. Jeff and Lizzy exemplify this dynamic. In the other situation, someone else has reactance to your efforts to influence their choices: for instance, Sally facing Lizzy's reactant behavior.

One effective debiasing technique for reactance involves *considering alternative explanations and options*. The inherent nature of reactance involves opposition to a perception of an external authority limiting one's options. The autopilot response focuses on doing the exact opposite of what the external authority endorses. However, many alternative options exist besides the obvious inverse.

For instance, Lizzy might have considered the option of talking to her mother about how she felt about the attack on Mark, instead of defending him. She might have shared that the attack on Mark made her feel like her mom was trying to run her whole life, by cutting off the first major independent initiative she took. Lizzy could have pointed out that she wanted more freedom and autonomy as she reached maturity, asking Sally to stop treating her like a kid. Lizzy might have considered making a deal with Sally, agreeing that as long as she kept up her grades and civic involvement—both were important for Sally due to the focus placed by colleges on a combination of grades and extracurricular activities—that Sally would give her the freedom to date whoever she wanted.

In turn, Jeff could have deployed an alternative perspective of looking at marriage even before the political tribulations in 2016. Instead of seeing marriage as a mechanism for social conformity, he could have looked at it from the perspective of goal achievement. Namely, he could have evaluated whether getting married would serve his overarching life goals as opposed to not getting married, making a list of pros and cons for each option. He told me later that if he actually sat down and evaluated this question long before the 2016 election, he would have chosen to wed his long-term girlfriend much earlier. So is there anything in your relationships or other life areas that you should reevaluate right now with an alternative perspective, before a personal, community, or political upheaval forces you to do so?

The other relevant debiasing strategy is *reflecting on the long-term future and on repeating scenarios*. Sally might have observed that her repeated criticism of Mark did not lead to her desired outcome, instead worsening her relationship due to Lizzy's reactance. Sally could have considered what would happen in the future if she kept repeating the same behaviors. With that in mind, she might have recognized that for the sake of her future relationship with Lizzy, she should stop simply disparaging her daughter's romantic choices.

Instead, Sally might have oriented toward the long term, when her daughter would be a fully independent adult, and launched a mature conversation. Sally could have asked with curiosity and empathy what inspired Lizzy to date Mark, given their obvious differences. Opening that dialogue would give Sally a chance to grasp that Lizzy had been feeling increasingly frustrated over Sally's somewhat domineering parenting style as Lizzy grew up and acquired a greater sense of autonomy. Understanding more about Lizzy's emotions, Sally could have displayed emotional maturity and worked out more effective ways of parenting Lizzy using her intentional system, instead of just parenting on autopilot as unfortunately so many parents do (not a dig at you, Mom and Dad, don't need to call me and complain).

Solving Reactance Exercise

Please take a few minutes to journal your answers to these questions before going onward:

- How will you use *considering alternative explanations and options* to fight reactance, whether in yourself and/or in others around you? Specifically, how will you implement this strategy? What challenges do you anticipate seeing in this implementation, and how will you overcome these challenges? What metrics will you use to measure your success in implementing this approach? What would the future of your relationships look like if you succeed in your implementation?

- How will you use *reflecting on the long-term future and on repeating scenarios* to help you address reactance, in yourself or in others around you? Specifically, how will you implement this strategy? What challenges do you anticipate seeing in this implementation, and how will you overcome these challenges? What metrics will you use to measure your success in implementing this approach? What would the future of your relationships look like if you succeed in your implementation?

Authority Bias

Just like optimism bias has its opposite in the form of pessimism bias, reactance has its opposite: the "authority bias," also called the "obedience bias." This bias describes our susceptibility to give more weight to and obey those we perceive as authorities than we objectively should.[110]

Just like it benefitted the tribe for at least some members to show reactance, it also proved necessary for even more tribe members—the large majority, in all likelihood—to obey the authority of the leadership. Tribes often had to make difficult and vital decisions quickly, and the survival of the tribe depended just as much, or even more, on the cohesion of the large majority than on the accuracy of the decision. Maintaining unity—even if you personally opposed the tribe's decision—helped you survive, given that in the content of the savanna, if you got kicked out of the tribe, you died. No wonder that most people today have an excessive predisposition to obey those with authority.

Take Ryiadha as an example. She felt some back and neck pain for a month, which she brought up to her friend and family doctor, Deepa. Deepa couldn't figure out the problem and sent her to Mark, an orthopedic doctor, recommending him highly. Mark examined Ryiadha and found that she had two spinal disks that had degenerated, confidently diagnosing these as the cause.

Mark brought up spinal fusion surgery as an option, saying it's the best cure for degenerative disk disease. He underscored that physical therapy might help with the pain but wouldn't address the underlying root of the problem. Ryiadha wanted the problem gone. Trusting Mark as a credible authority due to the referral from Deepa, Ryiadha agreed to go under the knife. After an expensive surgery, costing $4,300 with insurance, Ryiadha spent three months recovering and doing physical therapy.

Yet the previous pain persisted, together with the new pain from the surgery. Ryiadha felt pretty unhappy with the outcome, casting around for what to do. A friend recommended she try an ergonomics specialist, whose expertise involves observing how people interact with their physical environment, especially in the workplace, to address any potential problems. The ergonomics specialist came to observe her workplace at the job she started a couple of months prior, finding that the positioning of her keyboard, mouse, and computer screen caused her to move in ways that facilitated neck and back pain. After changing her setup, the original pain disappeared rapidly.

Frustrated with her friend, as well as with Mark, Ryiadha decided to investigate degenerated discs. She found that in many cases, degenerated discs cause no pain; even if they do, the pain usually decreases or completely disappears in a few months.[111] Moreover, patients with less costly nonsurgical treatments do about as well as patients with surgical treatment in the long term.[112] Unfortunately, many less scrupulous orthopedic doctors push patients whose discs look worn-out to have surgery as this expensive procedure offers surgeons the biggest financial and reputational gain, regardless of whether such surgery actually helps the patient.[113] Finding this out severely harmed Ryiadha's friendship with and trust of Deepa, not to speak of Mark.

Authority Bias Exercise

Please take out your journal, and spend a few minutes writing down your answers to these questions:

- Where have you fallen into *authority bias* in your life? How has doing so harmed your relationships? Where have you seen other people fall for this cognitive bias in their lives? How has doing so harmed their relationships?

Solving Authority Bias

In solving the authority bias, it helps to draw on both of the debiasing methods mentioned earlier, considering alternative explanations and options as well as reflecting on the long-term future and repeating scenarios. Yet two more methods offer even better options.

First, make sure to deploy the debiasing strategy of *probabilistic thinking*. Much of the trouble with authority bias stems from two elements: first, giving too much trust to the accuracy of authority figures and second, overestimating the extent to which complying with authority figures benefits you. If you know yourself to be susceptible to authority bias, as most people are, make sure to use your intentional system to estimate both of these elements.

What should Ryiadha have done after receiving a diagnosis of a serious medical condition for her neck and back pain, along with a recommendation of surgery? First, she should have evaluated the general accuracy of doctors making medical diagnoses. On average, medical doctors misdiagnose all conditions between 10 to 15 percent of the time.[114] What if we focus only on serious medical conditions like the one suffered by Riyadh, which tend to be harder to diagnose? A study by the world-renowned Mayo Clinic found that serious medical conditions were misdiagnosed 21 percent of the time, and 66 percent were incompletely diagnosed.[115] Overconfidence effect, the cognitive bias covered earlier in the book, is a major cause of misdiagnoses.[116]

Given this base rate—the initial probability of something occurring without any further evidence—Ryiadha should have used probabilistic thinking to be somewhat skeptical of Mark's diagnosis. It would have been wise to get a second opinion, preferably from a different type of medical doctor who does not specialize in surgery, such as a pain management specialist.

Then, Riyadh should have added to her evidence base by doing the research she ended up doing more than three months after her surgery. With that research, she would have discovered many more reasons to be skeptical, both of Mark's diagnosis and especially his aggressive—and expensive—treatment suggestion.

An additional debiasing method related to probabilistic thinking involves *making predictions about the future*. With the gathered evidence, she should have evaluated the possible futures. First, she could have predicted whether or not the pain was actually due to the degenerated disks. She could have explored this question by evaluating any changes that occurred recently, such as getting her new job. That change could have led her to turn to an ergonomics specialist much sooner. Second, even if the pain was due to the worn-out disks, which it apparently wasn't, she could have predicted whether the pain would go away on its own, as is often the case for worn-out disks, in a couple of months. Third, if the pain did not go away, she could have predicted whether less aggressive treatments would have addressed the pain and, based on the research, could have been quite confident that spinal fusion would not serve her needs.

This combination of probabilistic thinking and making predictions can serve you well when dealing with authority figures. For instance, research on expert predictions shows experts overwhelmingly suffer from overconfidence.[117] Some show more overconfidence and bad judgment than others: weather forecasters make more accurate predictions than financial analysts.[118] Overall, your base rate for expert opinions should be to consider the expert to be at least somewhat overconfident and to decrease your confidence in the accuracy of their conclusions. Similarly, if you're an authority figure yourself, remember that others will tend to put too much trust into what you say, so you should calibrate accordingly.

Solving Authority Bias Exercise

Please take a few minutes to journal your answers to these questions before going onward:

- How will you use *probabilistic thinking* to solve authority bias? Specifically, how will you implement this strategy? What challenges do you anticipate seeing in this implementation, and how will you overcome these challenges? What metrics will you use to measure your success in implementing this approach? What would the future of your relationships look like if you succeed in your implementation?

- How will you use *predicting the future* to help you address authority bias? Specifically, how will you implement this strategy? What challenges do you anticipate seeing in this implementation, and how will you overcome these challenges? What metrics will you use to measure your success in implementing this approach? What would the future of your relationships look like if you succeed in your implementation?

Conclusion

It may feel ironic and contradictory that your relationships—and your life as a whole—may be harmed just as much from listening to authority as from rebelling against authority. In both cases, too much of a good thing is bad for you. You have to seek that golden middle, by being aware of your own predilections and taking the steps necessary to correct for them.

Jeff's story offers a vision of a successful model of doing so. He reassessed his life choices in the context of a time of political upheaval. Recognizing his past mistakes, he didn't flinch away from taking the hard step of updating his beliefs through using the debiasing method of considering alternative explanations and options. Sure, he could have done so earlier, and wishes he would have. Still, so many people fail to take advantage of potentially life-changing moments to change their lives. A case in point, only a small proportion of all people who suffer a heart attack adhere to medical guidelines to prevent a second one: for instance, of all smokers, only 52 percent managed to quit, despite the increased risk of dying.[119]

You don't need to suffer such a wake-up call. Assess your life right now and see where your relationships and other areas might be suffering due to reactance or authority bias. Deploy the effective debiasing strategies described in this chapter to protect yourself. For more ideas on debiasing yourself from authority bias, reactance, and other cognitive biases, turn to this book's website: http://disasteravoidanceexperts.com/blindspots.

So far, this book has focused on helping you avoid disasters in your relationships and more broadly through addressing dangerous judgment errors mainly within yourself. Yet what happens when you observe others behaving irrationally, failing to believe the facts due to emotional blocks, often under the influence of the kind of cognitive biases described so far? Arguing with them won't help. The next chapter provides an effective communication strategy to help those you care about believe the facts and recognize and address the dangerous judgment errors from which they're suffering.

CHAPTER 9

Communicating Rationally

Michelle was having fun at her girlfriend Sharon's birthday party, talking with Sharon's other friends and family. Sharon warned Michelle that some of her family had outlandish views, but so far, Michelle didn't see any signs of that.

However, the situation changed when Michelle began talking to Mike, Sharon's brother. The conversation turned toward recent political developments, namely rising hate crimes against Muslims and the call from some conservative politicians to police Muslims heavily. To Michelle's shock, Mike endorsed both vigilante violence and heavy-handed policing of Muslims, telling Michelle, "Not all Muslims are terrorists, but all terrorists are Muslims."

Michelle's jaw dropped when she heard that. As a police officer, she knew Mike was thoroughly mistaken, as were the many other people who held that attitude.[120] She told him that an FBI study that evaluated terrorism in the US between 1980 and 2005 (which included 9/11) discovered that Muslims committed only 6 percent of all terrorist attacks.[121] Mike countered her, saying that only Muslims committed true terrorism, that the others shouldn't count as terrorist attacks. They began to argue, getting more and more heated. Regardless of the fact that Michelle had the facts on her side, she couldn't convince him: Mike kept doubling down on his inaccurate claims. Michelle's mood quickly soured, and she left the party. Later, she heard from Sharon that Mike, who got increasingly tipsy, talked trash about her to other party guests, misrepresenting her position and falsely claiming she supported Muslim terrorists.

Heated arguments with people who hold irrational beliefs—meaning beliefs that go against the facts—almost never lead to such people changing their mind. Instead, such debates often lead to hurt feelings and damaged relationships. This chapter offers an effective strategy of convincing people who hold irrational beliefs, usually due to a variety of cognitive biases, to change their minds to align with the truth of reality.

The Problem with Debates

As a teenager, I was one of the best in my school at debates. Hanging out with other intellectually oriented kids on the math team, otherwise known as the "nerd club," we argued constantly. It was our way of competing, establishing dominance, and feeling good about ourselves. We took IQ tests and competed with each other for the highest score. We showed off in class by trying to give the best answers and nitpicking the answers given by other students. Sure, we got beaten up after school by the jocks, but we beat them in class, and the teachers loved us.

My experience matches that of many others who found pride and meaning in their high intelligence and debate skills. It was only after I started to read the research on debating once I attended graduate school that I realized the problem with debates. A prominent evolutionary psychologist theorized that we evolved the capacity to argue not with the intention to figure out the truth, but with the intention to win for our own side in social conflicts within tribes on the ancient savannah.[122]

Reading about this thesis helped me realize some problematic aspects of debating. I know many smart people who posit that debates are the best way of figuring out the truth. However, let's be honest with each other. How many times have you argued for a position you had doubts about? Heck, I remember arguing in school for why Coke was better than Snapple as part of a class debate and winning that debate—and I much prefer Snapple to Coke (Snapple did not pay me for this endorsement). In fact, many of my classmates were genuinely shocked afterward that I actually argued so well for a position that differed from my own.

Indeed, there's a reason that rhetoric is a skill taught in college classes and why publishers print so many books about how to win arguments. Debating is a skill, and while winning a debate is easier if you have the truth on your side, skilled debaters can easily win over those who have weaker skills, even if the other's perspective is closer to the truth. In fact, research shows that participating in debates does not reduce certain cognitive biases, such as the tendency to look for and evaluate evidence with a bias toward one's current opinion.[123]

In addition to winning the argument for their side, people have many other motivations for debate besides seeking the truth. Some debate as a mode of entertainment and enjoyment. To me and plenty other people, it feels exciting and fun to cross intellectual swords with a worthy opponent, to parry and riposte. There's nothing like finding weaknesses in my opponent's arguments and striking hard, piercing their defenses and landing a solid blow, while blocking their attacks on my weak points.

Did you notice all of the metaphors I used for debate as warfare above? If not, it's because of how our structure of language leads us to accept naturally such metaphors as appropriate.[124] If we think of debate as a fight where we win or lose based on whether our argument prevails, we are not very likely to seek out the truth. How easy do you think it is to acknowledge a worthwhile point made by an opponent in a debate if I am seeking to protect myself from his strikes while marshalling my forces to make a strong counterblow?

Another reason to avoid debate when seeking to find the truth springs from the gender imbalance in debating. Women tend to avoid competition, while men seek it, according to research.[125] Thus, women tend to avoid participating in a debate-oriented interaction, regardless of whether their perspective matches reality more closely. To ensure that women's voices get truly heard, men should minimize and ideally avoid debating, especially around emotionally inflected topics.

The problems with debates don't necessarily imply we should not argue—far from it. However, I suggest not overloading people who hold irrational beliefs with facts that oppose their beliefs because research shows is a very poor way to reach them.[126] That's what Michelle tried to do with Mike—and probably what you have tried to do in the past—and it generally doesn't work. Even more problematically, sometimes trying to correct someone's false beliefs may backfire by increasing their perceptions that the false beliefs are true.[127]

Instead, I suggest focusing on reaching them emotionally in a way that gets to the heart of their beliefs through their autopilot system. Please note: The method described below works only in the case when the people with whom you're speaking hold a belief that's countered by clearly observable facts. Do not try to use it in contexts where the facts are under serious dispute (Is free trade good for American workers?), or where the disagreement centers on questions of value (Is abortion right or wrong?), or in matters of personal preference (keeping the thermostat at 69 degrees or 75 degrees).

Debates Exercise

You might want to argue about doing these exercises. Avoid that autopilot system temptation: it's not guiding you to behave rationally. Instead, please take out your journal, and spend a few minutes writing down your answers to these questions:

- How often do you argue with people holding irrational beliefs, beliefs clearly contradicted by the facts? How have you benefitted from such arguments? How have such arguments hurt you? In what percentage of cases did the people you argued with change their mind? How have these arguments impacted your relationships with these people and with others as well?

Don't Argue, EGRIP Instead!

When someone denies a clearly observable fact supported by clearly observable evidence, it's very likely that an emotional block is in play. That applies to social and cultural issues, such as falsely claiming that all terrorists are Muslims or believing that vaccines cause autism, and everyday life issues, such as a business leader failing to acknowledge uncomfortable facts about a company's performance or your grandma denying her vision is so bad that she shouldn't drive. Due to one or more cognitive biases, either the ones discussed in this book or the many dozens of others that I didn't have space to cover, the person's autopilot system leads them to turn away from the truth.[128] If you pressure them by presenting the facts, they will experience your efforts to correct their misconceptions—however well intended—as an attack. They will respond with their fight or flight instinct, either arguing back or shutting down and ignoring you.

Instead, use a research-driven methodology to help correct the other person's failure to see reality clearly. An excellent way to do so is a five-step approach I devised, tested, and use extensively, which can be summarized under the acronym EGRIP, which stands for emotions, goals, rapport, information, and positive reinforcement.[129]

EGRIP Case Study:
Muslims and Terrorism

Step 1: Emotions

If someone denies clear facts, you can safely assume that it's their emotions that are leading them away from reality. You need to deploy the skill of empathy, meaning understanding other people's emotions, to determine what emotional blocks might cause them to deny reality.[130]

In Mike's case, it's relatively easy to figure out the emotions at play through making a guess based on what research shows about what more conservative people who support persecuting Muslims value: security.[131] Michelle could have confirmed this guesstimate through active listening and using empathetic curiosity to question Mike about his concerns about Muslims. He would likely share extensively about his fears of all Muslims being potential terrorists, explaining his desire to lash out at them based on his desire to defend himself and others.

Step 2: Goals

Next, establish shared goals for both of you, which is crucial for effective knowledge sharing.[132] With Mike, Michelle could have talked about how they both want security for our society. She might choose to bring up her background as a police officer in discussing this point, pointing out her work in this field. Likewise, she would establish that they both want to commit to the facts, no matter where they lead us, as both want to avoid deceiving themselves and thus undermining their safety and security. This would be a good time to bring up Michelle's personal commitment to truthfulness through taking the Pro-Truth Pledge (at http://ProTruthPledge.org) and asking Mike to hold her accountable to the facts.[133] Doing so would help raise Michelle's credibility in Mike's eyes.

Step 3: Rapport

Third, build rapport. Using the empathetic listening you did previously, a vital skill in promoting trusting relationships, you would echo the other party's emotions and show that you understand how they feel. If possible, share a personal story where you felt such emotions to help them viscerally appreciate your emotional understanding.[134] In the case of Mike, Michelle would echo his fear and validate his emotions, telling him it's natural to feel afraid when we see Muslims committing terrorism, and it's where her gut reaction goes as well. She can share a story from her policing experience when she learned about a terrorist act committed by Muslims, describing how learning about it made her feel.

Step 4: Information

Now, move on to sharing information. Here is where you can give the facts that you held back in the beginning. Before sharing facts, it helps to point out that our emotions lead us astray. Try to use a contextual example based on the setting. For instance, Michelle could point to the large pack of cookies and the chips and dip at the party, saying that we might be tempted to indulge in junk food due to our instincts, but doing so would harm our health, so we need to moderate our instincts for the sake of our health goals.

Then, Michelle can move on to the facts about Muslims and terrorism. Here's where she can bring up the FBI study on Muslims and terrorism. Also, she can use probabilistic thinking to address safety concerns. For example, she can point out that there were eight terrorist acts in the US motivated in part by Islamic beliefs in 2016, with nine terrorists in total.[135] There are about 1.8 million Muslim adults in the US.[136] Thus, there's a one-in-two-hundred-thousand chance that any Muslim would commit a terrorist act in a given year. She can point out to Mike that's like picking out a terrorist randomly from the number of people in several football stadiums. From a policing perspective, Michelle can highlight that focusing efforts on surveilling Muslims will make us less secure by causing us to miss the actual terrorists.

In addition, she can note that the FBI praises Muslims for reporting threats.[137] Anti-Muslim vigilantism or government policies will make Muslims less likely to report threats. In fact, anti-Muslim political rhetoric by prominent US politicians is already being used to recruit terrorists in the US.[138] More anti-Muslim rhetoric and government policies will only result in more materials to recruit terrorists, Michelle can point out. The key here is to show your conversation partner, without arousing a defensive or aggressive response, how their current truth denialism will lead to them undermining the shared goals you both established earlier.[139]

Step 5: Positive Reinforcement

If you successfully carried out the steps described above, without inspiring a defensive or aggressive fight-or-flight response, the person is almost guaranteed to move—at least a little—toward facing reality. At this point, you'll want to offer positive reinforcement for their orientation toward the facts, a research-based tactic of altering the intuitive emotional habits of the auto-pilot system.[140] Effective positive reinforcement will not only help the other party stick with their new position on the matter of disagreement, but also make it more likely for them to update their beliefs toward the truth faster in the future.

With Michelle and Mike, if she's successful, Mike would agree that anti-Muslim policies and vigilantism seem unwise if we want to have more safety, regardless of how we intuitively feel. He would acknowledge that our society would be more secure if we are more tolerant and inclusive toward Muslims, even if his gut reactions make him uncomfortable with this recognition. Michelle can then support him—without being condescending—by saying that it's tough to make such uncomfortable realizations. She can share how she came to a similar perspective when learning about statistics on Muslims and terrorism from FBI training for local law enforcement, sharing her own surprise and discomfort. She can praise him for the broader principle of being willing to face emotionally uncomfortable facts, saying that many people wouldn't be able to make this difficult belief update.

Although your stories and feelings should be genuine, it's important to note that you don't have to experience emotions to the same extent as the people to whom you're speaking. For example, research shows that while liberals and conservatives generally share a similar range of emotions, the intensity of emotions differs radically. Conservatives have a much greater desire for safety and a more intense sense of tribalism.[141] Conservatives associate Muslims with danger and perceive them as outside their tribe: no wonder that they feel intense negative emotions toward Muslims. Yet even (non-Muslim) liberals may find within themselves at least a small part that feels fear about Muslim terrorism when they recall 9/11 and a sense that Muslims don't belong to their tribe. Sure, most liberals might immediately discard such feelings as contradicting their values, but when trying to convince conservatives, it's important to bring that part of yourself to the fore. The same, of course, would apply to conservatives who want to convince liberals who deny the facts, such as the well-known misconception, widespread among US liberals, that vaccines cause autism.[142]

Sounds manipulative? Step back and recognize that all of our social interactions with each other are manipulations of some sort or another. Some people are just naturally better at it than others: we call them "people with charisma" or "good salespeople." Using evidence-based methods like EGRIP—which only works when the person whom you're trying to convince holds false beliefs at odds with their own goals—you can use your intentional system to help those you speak to accept reality. And hey, if you ever see me holding mistaken beliefs, I urge you to use it on me as well!

You might feel skeptical that EGRIP can change the minds of well-informed conservatives. Let me give you an example of my radio interview with Scott Sloan, a prominent conservative radio show host on the radio station 700WLW. Sloan is popular enough and prominent enough that he had a friendly chat with Trump on his show during the election campaign. I went on his show soon afterward, on November 30, 2016, to talk about a terrorist attack at Ohio State University on November 28, 2016 by a Somali Muslim, Abdul Razak Ali Artan. He rammed his car into a crowd of students and then knifed several people before being shot dead by a university police officer.

Like many conservatives, Sloan associated Muslims with terrorism and wanted to persecute them harshly. I approached the ensuing discussion by considering his emotions and goals. I sought to meet him where he was, as opposed to where I would have liked him to be. I assessed that he valued safety and security first and foremost, and that he had negative feelings toward Muslims because he perceived them as a threat to safety and security. As we began talking, I validated the host's emotions, saying it was natural and intuitive in view of recent events to feel anger and fear toward Muslims, as our brains naturally take shortcuts by stereotyping groups based on the actions of one member of the group. However, such stereotyping often does not serve our actual goals and values.

I highlighted the statistics on Muslims described earlier in this chapter and that using "Muslim" as a filter for "terrorist" actually wastes our precious resources dedicated to safety and security and lets the real terrorists commit attacks. I also discussed the dangers of persecuting Muslims from the perspective of Muslim communities being less willing to help with terrorists in their midst, as well as more Muslims being willing to commit terrorist acts. In the end, Sloan agreed with my points and updated his views on Muslims, not because he felt like being generous toward Muslims, but because he valued his security and safety. I positively reinforced him for doing so. It's crucial to note that Sloan did so on live air, and his change of perspective likely influenced powerfully his many thousands of loyal listeners. A recording of the full interview is available for you to grasp the nuances and details of the technique.[143]

EGRIP Case Study: Workplace Denialism

A four-year study by LeadershipIQ.com interviewed 1,087 board members from 286 organizations of all sorts that had forced out their chief executive officers.[144] It found that 23 percent of CEOs were fired for denying reality, meaning refusing to recognize negative facts about their organization's performance. Other research shows that professionals at all levels of an organization suffer from the tendency to deny uncomfortable facts.[145] So how do you use EGRIP to get your peers, and especially your supervisors, to face reality?

I consulted for a company where a manager who made a hire refused to acknowledge the new employee's bad fit, despite everyone else in the department telling me that the employee was holding back the team. The HR VP asked me to help out as an uninvolved and neutral party. I started the conversation with this manager by discussing how she saw her current and potential future employees playing a role in the long-term future of her department. I echoed her anxiety about the company's performance and concerns about getting funding for future hires, which gave me an additional clue into why she might be protecting the incompetent employee.

Having understood the basics of her emotions and goals, I moved on to rapport. I shared a story from my past experience about other clients for whom tight budgets hindered recruiting, resulting in frustration and anxiety for them.

Next, I gently moved on to sharing information in a minimally threatening manner. I asked the manager to identify which of her employees contributed most to her goals for the department's long-term performance and which the least, and why. I also had her consider who contributed the most to the team spirit and unit cohesion and who dragged down morale and performance. As part of the conversation, I brought up research on why we sometimes make mistakes in evaluating employees and how to avoid them.[146] Additionally, I highlighted the damage done to the productivity and retention of quality employees by failing to address underperforming employees.[147]

She acknowledged the employee in question as being a poor performer and a drag on the group. Together, we collaborated on a plan of proactive development for the employee: if he did not meet agreed-upon benchmarks, he would be let go. I commended her for making a tough decision, one that requires unpleasant conversations and other forms of short-term pain for the sake of long-term benefit to her department. I noted that the best

business leaders are well-known and praised for accepting difficult facts to move forward, such as former Ford CEO Alan Mulally
helping save the company through repeated course
corrections.[148]

EGRIP Exercise

Please take a few minutes to journal your answers to these
questions before going onward:

- How will you use *EGRIP* to help people who hold
  irrational beliefs to acknowledge reality?
  Specifically, how will you implement this strategy?
  What challenges do you anticipate seeing in this
  implementation, and how will you overcome these
  challenges? What metrics will you use to measure
  your success in implementing this approach? What
  would the future of your relationships look like if
  you succeed in your implementation?

Conclusion

Michelle's frustrating interaction with Mike exemplifies the damaging consequences of trying to argue with irrational people who,
consciously or unconsciously, place their personal beliefs above
the facts. Her experience not only soured the party for her, but
also harmed her social status in Sharon's friendship circle. Such
futile arguments frequently lead to hurt feelings and damaged
relationships.

A wide variety of cognitive biases lead to such misconceptions, including many described in earlier chapters. Yet regardless
of which specific judgment error or combination of errors lead to
the irrational belief, you can use EGRIP to help you resolve the

issue. It only works when the person you're speaking to is indeed clearly and obviously in error. If you're not sure, ask an impartial objective external observer to use the known evidence to evaluate whether the case is open-and-shut or whether reasonable people can disagree; if it's the latter, don't use EGRIP.

The essence of this technique involves an empathetic, compassionate, and supportive conversation where you demonstrate to the other person that holding the false belief harms your shared goals. It's only possible where you identify genuine shared overarching goals: fortunately, it's quite easy to do so if you step back from the immediate matter at hand. After all, who doesn't want to be safe and secure? Which employee doesn't want the company to be profitable?

From the perspective of our shared humanity, we are all much more similar than different: we want a combination of peace, security, comfort, well-being, health, happiness, and social support. It's important to remember to focus on the other person's needs and wants, tapping into that part of yourself—however small—that resonates with them. I recommend practicing this technique in low-risk, low-intensity situations before using it on your boss or in a public radio interview, but as you improve, you can be confident about helping almost anyone who engages with you in good faith take steps—big or small—toward acknowledging reality and correcting their judgment errors. Other examples of using EGRIP are present on this book's website: http://disaster avoidanceexperts.com/blindspots.

Helping Others Spot Their Blindspots

Don't go in there, the monster is right behind the door! Have you ever had that thought when watching a horror movie? Well, now that you read this book, you might have this experience every time you see someone else falling into the mental blindspots described here.

I know that's how I began to think as I learned about them from reading recently published scientific papers cognitive biases and as I watched others around me harm their relationships due to these dangerous judgment errors. Of course, I had my own share of problems, as I began to think back—and cringe—at all the times my blindspots hurt me and others I cared about. I felt ashamed and guilty as I did exercises—much like the ones you've done throughout this book—and realized how my gut reactions undercut my relationships along with other life areas.

What helped me in getting these exercises done, despite my negative emotions, was the research clearly illustrating that to have any real hope of addressing cognitive biases, we need to recognize exactly how they have hurt us in the past and are harming us now. Only then can we lay the groundwork for solving these mental blindspots in the future, using the twelve debiasing strategies described in this book. Keep this book handy and turn to this chapter as a reminder of the twelve strategies, or refer to the first chapter for a fuller description of all of them:

1. Identifying your cognitive biases and making a plan to address them

2. Delaying your decisions and reactions

3. Probabilistic thinking

4. Making predictions about the future

5. Considering alternative explanations

6. Considering your past experiences

7. Reflecting on the future and repeating scenarios

8. Considering other people's points of view

9. Getting an external perspective

10. Setting a policy to guide your future self

11. Making a precommitment

12. Practicing mindfulness meditation

It's my hope that your desire to protect your relationships from further damage, and to see them not only survive but thrive in the future, has motivated you to complete all the exercises fully. If you haven't yet, please do go back and show self-care for yourself and compassion for others with whom you want to culti-vate healthy relationships by completing all the exercises. And if you want to help others in your life get rid of the irrational thought patterns that result from cognitive biases, make sure to learn, practice, and use EGRIP extensively.

A word of warning: avoid telling others what specific cognitive biases you notice them exhibiting. I wish someone conveyed that warning to my past self. A combination of the mental blindspots of *illusory superiority* (chapter 4) and *curse of knowledge* (chapter 5) did not serve me well when I initially learned about our mental blindspots. I came off to others as attacking them, and their autopilot systems responded with a defensive response even though I only wanted to help. That experience helped inspire my research on developing effective ways of helping others free themselves from irrational thought patterns, such as EGRIP.

Also, avoid the illusory superiority of believing yourself free from cognitive biases even once you learn about them. I had known about these dangerous judgment errors for over a decade before the serious conflicts with my wife in the winter and spring of 2014 when we started the nonprofit Intentional Insights and the tensions between my optimism bias and her pessimism bias came to the fore. As you experience life and relationship transitions, various cognitive biases will inevitably become more prominent while others weaken. Keep this book handy and reread it—and redo the exercises—as you and your loved ones undergo transitions.

A reminder that many more resources are available on the book's website: http://disasteravoidanceexperts.com/blindspots. I hope you will write to me and share your experiences with this book at gleb@disasteravoidanceexperts.com, and please leave a book review on Amazon and Goodreads. Get a copy for anyone in your life whose relationships you want to see survive and thrive.

If you take away one thing from this book, remember that what feels most comfortable is often exactly the wrong thing for the sake of healthy relationships. Our feelings of comfort—our autopilot system—is adapted for the ancestral savanna, when our survival depended on small tribes and powerful fight-or-flight responses. Yet our multicultural and globally interconnected present is very different from the ancestral savanna, and our technologically disrupted future is going to be even more distant from our tribal past. That ever-intensifying pace of change means our gut reactions will be less and less suited in the future and relying on our autopilot system will lead us to crash and burn in our relationships.

So I call on you to help your relationships not simply survive, but also flourish in the world of tomorrow by recognizing this paradigm shift and adopting the counterintuitive, uncomfortable, and successful intentional system debiasing techniques to address the systematic and predictable errors we all make. My best wishes to the health of your relationships and remember: you have much more ability to shape your relationships than you gut tells you!

Acknowledgments

Going against the grain of traditional relationship advice—which emphasizes following your gut, trusting your feelings, and going with your intuitions—can be a lonely journey. I am incredibly grateful to the many people who risked collaborating with me to depart from the mainstream and instead follow the counterintuitive revelations of cutting-edge research on avoiding dangerous judgment errors for the sake of helping their relationships survive and thrive. It's only thanks to their support that I can do my small part to address the deep suffering caused by people—who either followed their intuitions or trusted bad relationship advice—getting trapped by cognitive biases that damaged and sometimes ended their relationships.

First—both now and I hope always—I'm truly fortunate to have a life partner who is also my best friend, as well as business partner. I truly can't imagine my life without you, Agnes Vishnevkin. Your support, professional and personal, was the most important factor enabling me to write this book.

My thanks to the people who gave feedback on early versions of this book: you are too numerous to name. I'm thankful to David McRaney, who shared his thoughts in the foreword.

I greatly appreciate all the folks at New Harbinger who helped make this book happen. My particular gratitude goes to my editors—Elizabeth Hollis Hansen, Caleb Beckwith, and Wendy Millstine—whose wise advice on all aspects of my writing proved invaluable for the final product.

Finally, my thanks to you, the readers of this book. Without you reading it, my work has no meaning. I very much hope that your journey with this book will empower you to avoid the relationship disasters that result from falling into dangerous judgment errors and am eager to hear about your experience.

I take full responsibility for any mistakes: please bring them to my attention by emailing me at gleb@disasteravoidanceexperts.com. You can share other forms of feedback and more broadly your experience with the book by emailing me or visiting the book's website, http://www.disasteravoidanceexperts.com/blindspots, where you can submit your thoughts in a public post.

Glossary

Authority bias (also called the obedience bias): This cognitive bias describes our susceptibility to give more weight to and obey those we perceive as authorities than we objectively should.

Autopilot system: The older thinking and feeling system, which corresponds to our emotions, gut reactions, intuitions, and instincts. Centered around the amygdala in the brain, this system guides our daily habits, helps us make snap decisions, and reacts instantly to daily life situations, whether dangerous or not. It requires no effort to function and turns on in milliseconds. The autopilot system is prone to make systematic and predictable errors.

Blindspots: See cognitive biases.

Bystander effect: This cognitive bias refers to being much more willing to help people in a critical situation if we are the only one available to help. The more people witness an emergency and are available to help, the less likely we are to help and instead stand by while the emergency plays out.

Cognitive biases: The systematic and predictable dangerous judgment errors we tend to make in our relationships as well as other life areas. Many of these mental blindspots come from our evolutionary heritage. Certain judgment errors helped us survive in the savanna environment, such as overreacting to the presence of a perceived threat, but most do not serve us well in our modern environment. Other reasons for cognitive biases result from inherent limitations in our mental processing capacities, such as our difficulty keeping track of many varied data points. Most cognitive biases result from mistakes made by going with our gut reactions, meaning autopilot system errors. More rarely, cognitive biases are associated with intentional system errors.

Curse of knowledge: This cognitive bias refers to our difficulty remembering what it's like to not know what we now know about a topic. We often forget that other people don't know what we know, underestimate the difficulty of learning this information, and fail to communicate to others who don't know as much as we do about a topic effectively.

Egocentric bias: This cognitive bias is about our preference to ascribe to ourselves more credit than is actually due for the success of a collaborative project while blaming others for failures.

EGRIP: A research-driven methodology to help people who hold clearly irrational beliefs that are obviously at odds with reality get rid of the emotional blocks that limit their vision and help them see reality clearly. EGRIP is the acronym for the five steps of the process: (1) identifying the underlying *emotions* inhibiting the person from acknowledging the truth; (2) establishing shared *goals* for the two of you that would involve recognizing the facts; (3) building *rapport* through putting yourself into the same tribe and on the same side; (4) sharing *information* about a better way to reach your mutual goals by seeing reality clearly; (5) providing *positive reinforcement* when the other person shifts even a little toward seeing reality clearly.

Empathy gap: This cognitive bias refers to our tendency to underestimate the impact of emotions on other people as well as on ourselves during times of emotional arousal.

False consensus effect: This cognitive bias describes the fact that we greatly overestimate the extent to which our friends, family, colleagues, and all others agree with us, creating a sense of a false alignment with them in our head.

Fundamental attribution error (also called the correspondence bias): This cognitive bias involves our tendency to attribute (wrongly) the behaviors of other people to their personality and not to the context of the situation in which the behavior occurs.

Group attribution error: This cognitive bias describes our likelihood to perceive, wrongly, the characteristics of an individual member of a group to reflect the group as a whole or vice versa when we believe the group's overall preferences to determine the preferences of individuals within that group.

Halo effect: In this cognitive bias, when we feel a strong liking for one characteristic of someone, especially a trait that makes us feel like they're a part of a group to which we have a clear tribal affiliation, we will tend to have an excessively positive opinion of that person's other characteristics.

Horns effect: This cognitive bias refers to the fact that if we don't like some aspect of a person, particularly one that puts the individual in a group at odds with one to which we feel connected, we will evaluate that individual too harshly.

Illusion of transparency: This cognitive bias leads to us greatly overestimating the extent to which others perceive our feelings, thoughts, and beliefs.

Illusory superiority: This cognitive bias describes our predilection for overestimating our positive qualities and discounting negative ones.

Intentional system: The more recently evolved thinking system that reflects rational thinking and social judgment. It centers around the prefrontal cortex and helps us handle more complex mental activities, such as managing individual and group relationships, logical reasoning, probabilistic thinking, and learning new information and patterns of thinking and behavior. While the autopilot system requires no conscious effort to function, the intentional system requires a deliberate effort to turn on and is mentally tiring. We can train the intentional system to turn on in situations where the autopilot system is prone to make systematic and predictable errors.

Optimism bias: The cognitive bias of underestimating the likelihood of negative future events.

Overconfidence effect: The cognitive bias of feeling excessively confident about our evaluations of reality.

Pessimism bias: The cognitive bias of overestimating future dangers.

Reactance: The cognitive bias of feeling negative emotions when someone or something else limits our freedom of behavior or range of choices.

Social comparison bias: This cognitive bias refers to our tendency to compare ourselves to those we perceive as part of our tribe. We compete with each other in activities and possessions that bring social status, both one-upping gains made by others and, sadly, often tearing down others who have it better than us.

Ultimate attribution error: This cognitive bias causes us to misattribute problematic group behaviors to the internal characteristics of groups that we don't like as opposed to external circumstances and vice versa for groups we like.

Endnotes

Chapter 1

1   Raley, R. K., and L. Bumpass. 2003. "The Topography of the Divorce Plateau: Levels and Trends in Union Stability in the United States after 1980." *Demographic Research* 8: 245–260.

2   Olivola C. Y., and A. Todorov. 2010. "Fooled by First Impressions? Reexamining the Diagnostic Value of Appearance-Based Inferences." *Journal of Experimental Social Psychology* 46, no. 2: 315–324.

3   Rooth, D. O. 2010. "Automatic Associations and Discrimination in Hiring: Real World Evidence," *Labour Economics* 17, no. 3: 523–534.

4   Baert, S. 2010. "Hiring a Gay Man, Taking a Risk?: A Lab Experiment on Employment Discrimination and Risk Aversion." *Journal of Homosexuality* 65, no. 8: 1015–1031.

5   Shenkman, R. 2016. *Political Animals: How Our Stone-Age Brain Gets in the Way of Smart Politics.* New York: Basic Books.

6   Ariely, D. 2008. *Predictably Irrational: The Hidden Forces That Shape Our Decisions.* New York: HarperCollins.

7   Freud, S. 1949. *The Ego and the Id.* London: The Hogarth Press Ltd.

8   Kahneman, D. 2011. *Thinking, Fast and Slow.* New York: Farrar, Straus and Giroux.

9   Gigerenzer, G. 2007. *Gut Feelings: The Intelligence of the Unconscious.* New York: Penguin Books.

10 Haidt, J. 2007. *The Happiness Hypothesis: Putting Ancient Wisdom to the Test of Modern Science*. New York: Basic Books.

11 Heath, C., and D. Heath. 2001. *Decisive: How to Make Better Choices in Life and Work*. New York: Random House Business Books.

12 Job, V., C. S. Dweck, and G. M. Walton. 2010. "Ego Depletion—Is It All in Your Head? Implicit Theories about Willpower Affect Self-Regulation." *Psychological Science* 21, no. 11: 1686–1693.

13 Banaji, M. R., and A. G. Greenwald. 2016. *Blindspot: Hidden Biases of Good People*. New York: Delacorte Press.

14 Bond, C. F., and B. M. DePaulo. 2006. "Accuracy of Deception Judgments/" *Personality and Social Psychology Review* 10, no. 3: 214–234.

15 Mele, A. R. 1992. *Irrationality: An Essay on Akrasia, Self-Deception, and Self-Control*. Oxford: Oxford University Press.

16 Del Giudice, M. 2018. *Evolutionary Psychopathology: A Unified Approach*. Oxford: Oxford University Press.

17 Arkes, H. R. 1991. "Costs and Benefits of Judgment Errors: Implications for Debiasing." *Psychological Bulletin* 110, no. 3: 486–498.

18 Beaulac, G., and T. Kenyon. 2014. "Critical Thinking Education and Debiasing (Ailact Essay Prize Winner 2013)." *Informal Logic* 34, no. 4: 341–363.

19 Helmond, P., et al. 2015. "A Meta-Analysis on Cognitive Distortions and Externalizing Problem Behavior: Associations, Moderators, and Treatment Effectiveness." *Criminal Justice and Behavior* 42, no. 3: 245–262.

20 Lilienfeld, S. O., R. Ammirati, and K. Landfield. 2009. "Giving Debiasing Away: Can Psychological Research on Correcting Cognitive Errors Promote Human Welfare?" *Perspectives on Psychological Science* 4, no. 4: 390–398.

21 Cheng, F. F., and C. S Wu. 2010. "Debiasing the Framing Effect: The Effect of Warning and Involvement." *Decision Support Systems* 49, no. 3: 328–334.

22 Graf, L., et al. 2012. "Debiasing Competitive Irrationality: How Managers Can Be Prevented from Trading off Absolute for Relative Profit." *European Management Journal* 30, no. 4: 386–403.

23 Tetlock, P. E. 2017. *Expert Political Judgment: How Good Is It? How Can We Know?* Princeton, NJ: Princeton University Press.

24 Clemen, R. T., and K. C. Lichtendahl. 2002. "Debiasing Expert Overconfidence: A Bayesian Calibration Model." (Presentation at the Sixth International Conference on Probabilistic Safety Assessment and Management [PSAM6], June 27: 1–16.)

25 Flyvbjerg, B. 2008. "Curbing Optimism Bias and Strategic Misrepresentation in Planning: Reference Class Forecasting in Practice." *European Planning Studies* 16, no. 1: 3–21.

26 Tetlock, P. E., and D. Gardner. 2016. *Superforecasting: The Art and Science of Prediction.* New York: Random House.

27 Miller, A. K., et al. 2013. "Mental Simulation and Sexual Prejudice Reduction: The Debiasing Role of Counterfactual Thinking." *Journal of Applied Social Psychology* 43, no. 1: 190–194.

28 Kruger, J., and M. Evans. 2004. "If You Don't Want to Be Late, Enumerate: Unpacking Reduces the Planning Fallacy." *Journal of Experimental Social Psychology* 40, no. 5: 586–598.

29 Sanna, L. J., et al. 2005. "The Hourglass Is Half Full or Half Empty: Temporal Framing and the Group Planning Fallacy." *Group Dynamics: Theory, Research, and Practice* 9, no. 3: 173–188.

30 Galinsky, A. D. 1999. "Perspective-Taking: Debiasing Social Thought. (Stereotyping)." *Dissertation Abstracts International: Section B: The Sciences and Engineering* 60, no. 4-B: 708–724.

31 Rose, J. P. 2012. "Debiasing Comparative Optimism and Increasing Worry for Health Outcomes." *Journal of Health Psychology* 17, no. 8: 1121–1131.

32 Gawande, A. 2009. *The Checklist Manifesto: How to Get Things Right.* New York: Henry Holt and Company.

33 Tsipursky, G., F. Votta, and K. M. Roose. 2018. "Fighting Fake News and Post-Truth Politics with Behavioral Science: The Pro-Truth Pledge." *Behavior and Social Issues* 27, no. 2: 47–70.

34 Hafenbrack, A. C., Z. Kinias, and S. G. Barsade. 2014. "Debiasing the Mind through Meditation: Mindfulness and the Sunk-Cost Bias." *Psychological Science* 25, no. 2: 369–376.

35 Kabat-Zinn, J., and T. N. Hanh. 2009. *Full Catastrophe Living: Using the Wisdom of Your Body and Mind to Face Stress, Pain, and Illness.* Peaslake, UK: Delta.

Chapter 2

36 Gawronski, B. 2004. "Theory-Based Bias Correction in Dispositional Inference: The Fundamental Attribution Error Is Dead, Long Live the Correspondence Bias/" *European Review of Social Psychology* 15, no. 1: 183–217.

37 Bratman, G. N., et al. 2015. "Nature Experience Reduces Rumination and Subgenual Prefrontal Cortex Activation." *Proceedings of the National Academy of Sciences* 112, no. 28: 8567–8572.

38 Corneille, O., et al. 2001. "Threat and the Group Attribution Error: When Threat Elicits Judgments of Extremity and Homogeneity." *Personality and Social Psychology Bulletin* 27, no. 4: 437–446.

39 Hewstone, M. 1990. "The 'Ultimate Attribution Error'? A Review of the Literature on Intergroup Causal Attribution." *European Journal of Social Psychology* 20, no. 4: 311–335.

40 Fryer, R. G., Jr. 2018. "Reconciling Results on Racial Differences in Police Shootings." *AEA Papers and Proceedings* 108: 228–233.

41 Miller, R. J., L. J. Kern, and A. Williams. 2018. "The Front End of the Carceral State: Police Stops, Court Fines, and the Racialization of Due Process." *Social Service Review* 92, no. 2: 290–303.

42 Staats, C., et al. 2015. *State of the Science: Implicit Bias Review 2015*. Columbus: The Ohio State University.

43 Ross, H. J. 2011. *Reinventing Diversity: Transforming Organizational Community to Strengthen People, Purpose, and Performance*. Lanham, MD: Rowman & Littlefield.

44 Devine, P. G., et al. 2012. "Long-Term Reduction in Implicit Race Bias: A Prejudice Habit-Breaking Intervention." *Journal of Experimental Social Psychology* 48, no. 6: 1267–1278.

45 Dobbin F., and A. Kalev. 2016. "Why Diversity Programs Fail and What Works Better." *Harvard Business Review* 94, no. 7–8: 52–60.

46 Ross, H. J. 2018. *Our Search for Belonging: How Our Need to Connect Is Tearing Us Apart*. San Francisco: Berrett-Koehler.

Chapter 3

47 Whitman, W. 1994. *Leaves of Grass*. New York: Penguin Books.

48 Hornsey, M. J. 2003. "Linking Superiority Bias in the Interpersonal and Intergroup Domains." *The Journal of Social Psychology* 143, no. 4: 479–491.

49 Pulford, B. D., and A. M. Pulford. 1996. "Overconfidence, Base Rates and Outcome Positivity/Negativity of Predicted Events." *British Journal of Psychology* 87, no. 3: 431–445.

50 Savani, K. et al. 2014. "Culture and Judgment and Decision Making." *Handbook of Judgment and Decision Making*, 456–477.

51 Tsipursky, G., F. Votta, and K. M. Roose. 2018. "Fighting Fake News and Post-Truth Politics with Behavioral Science: The Pro-Truth Pledge." *Behavior and Social Issues* 27, no. 2: 47–70.

52 Finkelstein, S. 2004. *Why Smart Executives Fail: And What You Can Learn from Their Mistakes.* New York: Penguin Random House.

53 Chen, G., C. Crossland, and S. Luo. 2015. "Making the Same Mistake All Over Again: CEO Overconfidence and Corporate Resistance to Corrective Feedback." *Strategic Management Journal* 36, no. 10: 1513–1535.

54 Garcia, S. M., H. Song, and A. Tesser. 2010. "Tainted Recommendations: The Social Comparison Bias." *Organizational Behavior and Human Decision Processes* 113, no. 2: 97–101.

55 Vrangalova, Z., R. E. Bukberg, and G. Rieger. 2014. "Birds of a Feather? Not When It Comes to Sexual Permissiveness." *Journal of Social and Personal Relationships* 31, no. 1: 93–113.

56 DeLeire, T., and A. Kalil. 2010. "Does Consumption Buy Happiness? Evidence from the United States." *International Review of Economics* 57, no. 2: 163–176.

57 Gilovich, T., V. H. Medvec, and K. Savitsky. 2000. "The Spotlight Effect in Social Judgment: An Egocentric Bias in Estimates of the Salience of One's Own Actions and Appearance." *Journal of Personality and Social Psychology* 78, no. 2: 211–222.

Chapter 4

58 Burton, S., et al. 2015. "Broken Halos and Shattered Horns: Overcoming the Biasing Effects of Prior Expectations through Objective Information Disclosure." *Journal of the Academy of Marketing Science* 43, no. 2: 240–256.

59 Lippi-Green, R. 2012. *English with an Accent: Language, Ideology and Discrimination in the United States.* Abingdon, UK: Routledge.

60 Hoover, G. A., R. A. Compton, and D. C. Giedeman. 2015. "The Impact of Economic Freedom on the Black/White Income Gap." *American Economic Review* 105, no. 5: 587–592.

61 R. Pingitore, R., et al. 1994. "Bias against Overweight Job Applicants in a Simulated Employment Interview." *Journal of Applied Psychology* 79, no. 6: 909–917.

62 Carnevale, A. P., N. Smith, and A. Gulish. 2018. "Women Can't Win: Despite Making Educational Gains and Pursuing High-Wage Majors, Women Still Earn Less Than Men." Washington, DC: Georgetown University Center on Education and the Workforce, 1–68.

63 Higley, S. R. 1995. *Privilege, Power, and Place: The Geography of the American Upper Class.* Lanham, MD: Rowman & Littlefield.

64 Coombs, W. T., and S. J. Holladay. 2006. "Unpacking the Halo Effect: Reputation and Crisis Management." *Journal of Communication Management* 10, no. 2: 123–137.

65 Lucker, W. G., W. E. Beane, and R. L. Helmreich. 1981. "The Strength of the Halo Effect in Physical Attractiveness Research." *The Journal of Psychology* 107, no. 1: 69–75.

66 Eagly, A. H., et al. 1991. "What Is Beautiful Is Good, but…: A Meta-Analytic Review of Research on the Physical Attractiveness Stereotype." *Psychological Bulletin* 110, no. 1: 109–128.

67 Critelli, J. W., and L. R. Waid. 1980. "Physical Attractiveness, Romantic Love, and Equity Restoration in Dating Relationships." *Journal of Personality Assessment* 44, no. 6: 624–629.

68 Watkins, L. M., and L. Johnston. 2000. "Screening Job Applicants: The Impact of Physical Attractiveness and Application Quality." *International Journal of Selection and Assessment* 8, no. 2: 76–84.

69 Chiu, R. K., and R. D. Babcock. 2002. "The Relative Importance of Facial Attractiveness and Gender in Hong Kong Selection Decisions." *International Journal of Human Resource Management* 13, no. 1: 141–155.

70 French, M. T. 2002. "Physical Appearance and Earnings: Further Evidence." *Applied Economics* 34, no. 5: 569–572.

71 Judge, T. A., and D. M. Cable. 2004. "The Effect of Physical Height on Workplace Success and Income: Preliminary Test of a Theoretical Model." *Journal of Applied Psychology* 89, no. 3: 428–441.

72 Verhulst, B., M. Lodge, and H. Lavine. 2010. "The Attractiveness Halo: Why Some Candidates Are Perceived More Favorably Than Others." *Journal of Nonverbal Behavior* 34, no. 2: 111–117.

Chapter 5

73 Gilovich, T., and K. Savitsky. 1999. "The Spotlight Effect and the Illusion of Transparency: Egocentric Assessments of How We Are Seen by Others." *Current Directions in Psychological Science* 8, no. 6: 165–168.

74 Ekman, P., and M. O'Sullivan. 1991. "Who Can Catch a Liar?" *American Psychologist* 46, no. 9: 913–920.

75 Gilovich, T., K. Savitsky, and V. H. Medvec. 1998. "The Illusion of Transparency: Biased Assessments of Others' Ability to Read One's Emotional States." *Journal of Personality and Social Psychology* 75, no. 2: 332–346.

76 Van Boven, L., T. Gilovich, and V. H. Medvec. 2003. "The Illusion of Transparency in Negotiations." *Negotiation Journal* 19, no. 2: 117–131.

77 Furnham, A. 2003. "Belief in a Just World: Research Progress over the past Decade." *Personality and Individual Differences* 34, no. 5: 795–817.

78 Rosenberg, M. B., and A. Gandhi, *Nonviolent Communication: A Language of Life*. Encinitas, CA: Puddledancer Press.

79 Birch, S. A., and P. Bloom. 2007. "The Curse of Knowledge in Reasoning About False Beliefs." *Psychological Science* 18, no. 5: 382–386.

80 Coleman, M. D. 2018. "Emotion and the False Consensus Effect." *Current Psychology* 37, no. 1: 58–64.

81 Mannarini, T., M. Roccato, and S. Russo. 2015. "The False Consensus Effect: A Trigger of Radicalization in Locally

Unwanted Land Uses Conflicts." *Journal of Environmental Psychology* 42: 76–81.

82 Wojcieszak, M. E. 2011. "Computer-Mediated False Consensus: Radical Online Groups, Social Networks and News Media." *Mass Communication and Society* 14, no. 4: 527–546.

83 Wojcieszak, M., and V. Price. 2009. "What Underlies the False Consensus Effect? How Personal Opinion and Disagreement Affect Perception of Public Opinion." *International Journal of Public Opinion Research* 21, no. 1: 25–46.

84 Epley, N., et al. 2009. "Believers; Estimates of God's Beliefs Are More Egocentric Than Estimates of Other People's Beliefs." *Proceedings of the National Academy of Sciences* 106, no. 51: 21533–21538.

85 Welborn, B. L., and M. D. Lieberman. 2018. "Disconfirmation Modulates the Neural Correlates of the False Consensus Effect: A Parametric Modulation Approach." *Neuropsychologia* 121: 1–10.

Chapter 6

86 Schnall, S., J. Benton, and S. Harvey. 2008. "With a Clean Conscience: Cleanliness Reduces the Severity of Moral Judgments." *Psychological Science* 19, no. 12: 1219–1222.

87 Gutsell, J. N., and M. Inzlicht. 2012. "Intergroup Differences in the Sharing of Emotive States: Neural Evidence of an Empathy Gap." *Social Cognitive and Affective Neuroscience* 7, no. 5: 596–603.

88 Loewenstein, G. 2005. "Hot-Cold Empathy Gaps and Medical Decision Making." *Health Psychology* 24, no. 4S: S49–56.

89 Nordgren, L. F., K. Banas, and G. MacDonald. 2011. "Empathy Gaps for Social Pain: Why People Underestimate the Pain of Social Suffering." *Journal of Personality and Social Psychology* 100, no. 1: 120–128.

90 Broockman, D., and J. Kalla. 2016. "Durably Reducing Transphobia: A Field Experiment on Door-To-Door Canvassing," *Science* 352, no. 6282: 220–224.

91 Singer, P. 2015. "The Drowning Child and the Expanding Circle." *Focused Inquiry True Stories Narrative & Understanding*, 320–323.

92 Fischer, P., et al. 2011. "The Bystander-Effect: A Meta-Analytic Review on Bystander Intervention in Dangerous and Non-Dangerous Emergencies." *Psychological Bulletin* 137, no. 4: 517–537.

93 Van Bommel, M., et al. 2012. "Be Aware to Care: Public Self-Awareness Leads to a Reversal of the Bystander Effect." *Journal of Experimental Social Psychology* 48, no. 4: 926–930.

Chapter 7

94 Sharot, T., et al. 2012. "How Dopamine Enhances an Optimism Bias in Humans." *Current Biology* 22, no. 16: 1477–1481.

95 Johnson, D. D., and J. H. Fowler. 2011. "The Evolution of Overconfidence." *Nature* 477, no. 7364: 317–320.

96 Sharot, T. 2011. "The Optimism Bias." *Current Biology* 21, no. 23: R941–R945.

97 McKay, R. T., and D. C. Dennett. 2009. "The Evolution of Misbelief." *Behavioral and Brain Sciences* 32, no. 6: 493–510.

98 SBAOffice of Advocacy. 2012. "Do Economic or Industry Factors Affect Business Survival?" Retrieved from https://www.sba.gov/sites/default/files/Business-Survival.pdf.

99 Menon, G., E. J. Kyung, and N. Agrawal. 2009. "Biases in Social Comparisons: Optimism or Pessimism?" *Organizational Behavior and Human Decision Processes* 108, no. 1: 39–52.

100 McNamara, J. M., et al. 2011. "Environmental Variability Can Select for Optimism or Pessimism." *Ecology Letters* 14, no. 1: 58–62.

101 Alloy, L. B., and A. H. Ahrens. 1987. "Depression and Pessimism for the Future: Biased Use of Statistically Relevant Information in Predictions for Self Versus Others. " *Journal of Personality and Social Psychology* 52, no. 2: 366–378.

102 Schulz, R., et al. 2002. "Pessimism, Age, and Cancer Mortality." *Psychology and Aging* 11, no. 2: 304–309.

103 Helweg-Larsen, M., P. Sadeghian, and M. S. Webb. 2002. "The Stigma of Being Pessimistically Biased." *Journal of Social and Clinical Psychology* 21, no. 1: 92–107.

104 Norem, J. K., and K. S. Illingworth. 1993. "Strategy-Dependent Effects of Reflecting on Self and Tasks: Some Implications of Optimism and Defensive Pessimism." *Journal of Personality and Social Psychology* 65, no. 4: 822–835.

105 Norem, J. K., and N. Cantor, "Anticipatory and Post Hoc Cushioning Strategies: Optimism and Defensive Pessimism in "Risky" Situations." *Cognitive Therapy and Research* 10, no. 3: 347–362.

Chapter 8

106 Dubin, J. 2017. "How Trump Changed My Mind about Marriage." Retrieved from https://www.psychologytoday.com /us/blog/intentional-insights/201704/how-trump-changed -my-mind-about-marriage.

107 Brehm, S. S., and J. W. Brehm. 2013. *Psychological Reactance: A Theory of Freedom and Control.* Cambridge, MA: Academic Press.

108 Peper, J. S., and R. E. Dahl. 2013. "The Teenage Brain: Surging Hormones—Brain-Behavior Interactions During Puberty." *Current Directions in Psychological Science* 22, no. 2: 134–139.

109 Somerville, L. H. 2013. "The Teenage Brain: Sensitivity to Social Evaluation." *Current Directions in Psychological Science* 22, no. 2: 121–127.

110 Caprio, L. 2008. "How Can We Help Independent Directors to Escape the 'Obedience Bias'?" *Journal of Management & Governance* 12, no. 2: 201–204.

111 Deyo, R. A. 2007. "Back Surgery—Who Needs It." *New England Journal of Medicine* 356, no. 22: 2239–2243.

112 Jacobs, W. C., et al. 2011. "Surgery Versus Conservative Management of Sciatica Due to a Lumbar Herniated Disc: A Systematic Review." *European Spine Journal* 20, no. 4: 513–522.

113 Stahel, P. F., T. F. VanderHeiden, and F. J. Kim. 2017. "Why Do Surgeons Continue to Perform Unnecessary Surgery?" *Patient Safety in Surgery* 11, no. 1. https://pssjournal.biomed central.com/articles/10.1186/s13037-016-0117-6.

114 Graber, M. L. 2013. "The Incidence of Diagnostic Error in Medicine." *BMJ Quality & Safety* 22, no. Supplement 2: ii21–ii27.

115 an Such, M., et al. 2017. "Extent of Diagnostic Agreement Among Medical Referrals." *Journal of Evaluation in Clinical Practice* 23, no. 4: 870–874.

116 Berner, E. S., and M. L. Graber. 2008. "Overconfidence as a Cause of Diagnostic Error in Medicine." *The American Journal of Medicine* 121, no. 5: S2–S23.

117 Tetlock, P. E., and D. Gardner. 2016. *Superforecasting: The Art and Science of Prediction.* New York: Random House.

118 Tyszka, T., and P. Zielonka. 2002. "Expert Judgments: Financial Analysts Versus Weather Forecasters." *The Journal of Psychology and Financial Markets* 3, no. 3: 152–160.

119 Choi, Y. J., et al. 2013. "Changes in Smoking Behavior and Adherence to Preventive Guidelines among Smokers After a Heart Attack." *Journal of Geriatric Cardiology: JGC* 10, no. 2: 146–150.

Chapter 9

120 Green, T. H. 2018. *Presumed Guilty: Why We Shouldn't Ask Muslims to Condemn Terrorism.* Minneapolis, MN: Fortress Press.

121 FBI. *Terrorism in the United States, 2002–2005.* Retrieved from https://www.fbi.gov/stats-services/publications/terrorism -2002-2005#terror_05sum, 2006.

122 Kurzban, R. 2011. *Why Everyone (Else) Is a Hypocrite: Evolution and the Modular Mind.* Princeton: Princeton University Press.

123 Perkins, D., B. Bushey, and M. Fararady. 1986. *Learning to Reason.* Cambridge, MA: Harvard Graduate School of Education.

124 Lakoff, G., and M. Johnson. 1980. *Metaphors We Live By.* Chicago: University of Chicago Press.

125 Niederle, M., and L. Vesterlund. 2007. "Do Women Shy Away from Competition? Do Men Compete Too Much?" *The Quarterly Journal of Economics* 122, no. 3: 1067–1101.

126 Flynn, D. J., B. Nyhan, and J. Reifler. 2017. "The Nature and Origins of Misperceptions: Understanding False and Unsupported Beliefs About Politics." *Political Psychology* 38: 127–150.

127 Peter, C., and T. Koch. 2016. "When Debunking Scientific Myths Fails (and When It Does Not) the Backfire Effect in the Context of Journalistic Coverage and Immediate Judgments as Prevention Strategy." *Science Communication* 38, no. 1: 3–25.

128 Kahneman, D. 2011. *Thinking, Fast and Slow.* New York: Farrar, Straus and Giroux.

129 Tsipursky, G. 2017. "How Can Facts Trump Ideology?" *The Human Prospect* 6, no. 4: 4–10.

130 Mayer, J.D., and G. Geher. 1996. "Emotional Intelligence and the Identification of Emotion." *Intelligence* 22, no. 2: 89–113.

131 Haidt, J. 2012. *The Righteous Mind: Why Good People Are Divided by Politics and Religion.* New York: Vintage.

132 Ames, C. 1992. "Classrooms: Goals, Structures, and Student Motivation." *Journal of Educational Psychology* 84, no. 3: 261–271.

133 Tsipursky, G., F. Votta, and J. A. Mulick. 2018. "A Psychological Approach to Promoting Truth in Politics: The Pro-Truth Pledge." *Journal of Social and Political Psychology* 6, no. 2: 271–290.

134 Aggarwal, P. 2005. "Salesperson Empathy and Listening: Impact on Relationship Outcomes." *Journal of Marketing Theory and Practice* 13, no. 3: 16–31.

135 Johnston, W. R. 2018. "Terrorist Attacks and Related Incidents in the United States." Retrieved from http://www.johnstonsarchive.net/terrorism/wrjp255a.html.

136 Pew Research Center. 2011. "Section 1: A Demographic Portrait of Muslim Americans." Retrieved from https://www.people-press.org/2011/08/30/section-1-a-demographic-portrait-of-muslim-americans/.

137 Cooke, K., and J. Ax. 2016. "US Officials Say American Muslims Do Report Extremist Threats." *Reuters.* Retrieved from https://www.reuters.com/article/us-florida-shooting-cooperation/u-s-officials-say-american-muslims-do-report-extremist-threats-idUSKCN0Z213U.

138 Howell. K. 2016. "Donald Trump Appears in Al-Shabab's New Terrorism Recruiting Video." *The Washington Times.* Retrieved from https://www.washingtontimes.com/news/2016/jan/2/donald-trump-appears-in-new-terrorism-recruiting-v/.

139 Arkes, H. R. 1991. "Costs and Benefits of Judgment Errors: Implications for Debiasing." *Psychological Bulletin* 110, no. 3: 486–498.

140 Kamery, R. H. 2004. "Motivation Techniques for Positive Reinforcement: A Review." *Allied Academies International Conference. Academy of Legal, Ethical and Regulatory Issues. Proceedings* 8, no. 2: 91–96.

141 Haidt, J., J. Graham, and C. Joseph. 2009. "Above and Below Left-Right: Ideological Narratives and Moral Foundations." *Psychological Inquiry* 20, no. 2–3: 110–119.

142 DeStefano, F. 2007. "Vaccines and Autism: Evidence Does Not Support a Causal Association." *Clinical Pharmacology & Therapeutics* 82, no. 6: 756–759.

143 Tsipursky, G. 2016. "Responding Rationally to the Ohio State Terrorist Attack: A Conservative Take." Retrieved from https://www.spreaker.com/user/gleb_tsipursky/responding -rationally-to-the-ohio-state-.

144 Murphy, M. 2005. "Leadership IQ Study: Mismanagement, Inaction among the Real Reasons Why CEOs Get Fired." Retrieved from http://www.prweb.com/releases/200s5/06/pr web253465.htm.

145 Tedlow, R. S. 2010. *Denial: Why Business Leaders Fail to Look Facts in the Face—And What to Do About It.* New York: Penguin.

146 Highhouse, S. 2008. "Stubborn Reliance on Intuition and Subjectivity in Employee Selection." *Industrial and Organizational Psychology* 1, no. 3: 333–342.

147 Self, D. R., and T. B. Self. 2014. "Negligent Retention of Counterproductive Employees." *International Journal of Law and Management* 56, no. 3: 216–230.

148 Hoffman, B. G. 2012. *American ICON: Alan Mulally and the Fight to Save Ford Motor Company.* New York: Three Rivers Press.

Gleb Tsipursky, PhD, is a cognitive neuroscientist and behavioral economist on a mission to protect people from relationship disasters caused by the mental blindspots known as cognitive biases through the use of cognitive behavioral therapy (CBT)-informed strategies. His expertise comes from over fifteen years in academia researching cognitive neuroscience and behavioral economics, including seven as a professor at Ohio State University, where he published dozens of peer-reviewed articles in academic journals such as *Behavior and Social Issues* and *Journal of Social and Political Psychology*. It also stems from his background of over twenty years of consulting, coaching, speaking, and training on improving relationships in business settings as CEO of Disaster Avoidance Experts.

A civic activist, Tsipursky leads Intentional Insights, a nonprofit organization popularizing the research on solving cognitive biases, and has extensive expertise on translating the research to a broad audience. His cutting-edge thought leadership was featured in over 400 articles and 350 interviews in *Time, Scientific American, Psychology Today, Newsweek, The Conversation,* CNBC, CBS News, NPR, and more. A best-selling author, he wrote *Never Go With Your Gut, The Truth Seeker's Handbook,* and *Pro Truth.* He lives in Columbus, OH; and to avoid disaster in his personal life, makes sure to spend ample time with his wife.

Foreword writer **David McRaney** is an internationally best-selling author, journalist, and lecturer who created the *You Are Not So Smart* books and blog, which cover the psychology of reasoning, biases, delusions, and fallacies. He has appeared as himself in a national ad campaign for Reebok, and his writing has been featured in campaigns for Heineken and Duck Tape, among others. David currently hosts the *You Are Not So Smart* podcast, and travels around the planet giving lectures on how we are the unreliable narrators in the stories of our lives.

Real change *is* possible

For more than forty-five years, New Harbinger has published proven-effective self-help books and pioneering workbooks to help readers of all ages and backgrounds improve mental health and well-being, and achieve lasting personal growth. In addition, our spirituality books offer profound guidance for deepening awareness and cultivating healing, self-discovery, and fulfillment.

Founded by psychologist Matthew McKay and Patrick Fanning, New Harbinger is proud to be an independent, employee-owned company. Our books reflect our core values of integrity, innovation, commitment, sustainability, compassion, and trust. Written by leaders in the field and recommended by therapists worldwide, New Harbinger books are practical, accessible, and provide real tools for real change.

 **newharbinger**publications

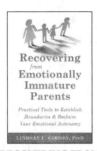

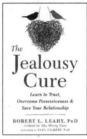
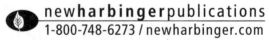